BENN'S WORLD HISTORIES

Russia of the Tsars

1796-1917

DAVID SMITH

LONDON   ERNEST BENN LIMITED   1971

First published 1971 by Ernest Benn Limited
Bouverie House, Fleet Street, London EC4

© *David Smith 1971*

Book designed by Kenneth Day
Maps by K. J. Wass

Distributed in Canada by
The General Publishing Company Limited, Toronto

Printed in Great Britain

ISBN 0-510-18410-3

Title page

1   The 'Montagne Russe'—a very dangerous game

Contents

Maps

1 Tsars and Serfs

Very soon the cobbled roadway came to an end, the barrier was passed, the town lay behind, and nothing remained but the journey ahead. And here he was again on the highway, with the milestones flashing past him on both sides of the road, together with posting-stations, wells, caravans, drab villages with samovars, peasant women and a rugged bearded inn-keeper, who was running out of a coaching yard with a heap of oats in his arms; a tramp in worn bast-shoes tramping along his five hundred miles; little towns, haphazardly built, with wooden stores, barrels of flour, bast-shoes, calatches and other assortments; black and white barriers, bridges under repair, endless fields and, coming and going on either side of him, antique landowners' carriages, a soldier on horseback carrying a green box full of lead peas with the name of a certain battery inscribed upon it; green, yellow and black, freshly ploughed strips flashing in the steppes; a song rising in the distance, the tops of pine trees through the mist, the fading sound of ringing bells, crows as thick as flies and an illimitable horizon . . . Russia! Russia!

NICHOLAS GOGOL: *Dead Souls*

THIS VIVID DESCRIPTION of a Russian scene comes from the pen of a novelist who has been described as the Russian Dickens. Crowded and busy though the picture is, the overriding impression is of the poverty and backwardness of this great country to the east of Europe. The villages are drab and primitive. The social differences are obvious and great, but even the landowners' carriages are old and shabby. Above all, perhaps, Gogol evokes the vast and brooding emptiness of the steppes of southern Russia. Like the prairies of America, these almost treeless plains stretched endlessly and monotonously as far as the eye could see. Like the prairies, the steppes were fertile, watered by the great rivers Don and Volga. In winter however snow-bearing winds swept relentlessly across them. It was a hard land, whose overpowering landscape reduced men and their works to insignificance. Towns and villages, in Gogol's phrase, were 'like dots, marks imperceptibly stuck upon the plains'. It is not too fanciful to detect some connection between this melancholy landscape and the character of its inhabitants. They also tended to be sad and brooding, conscious of their insignificance in the face of nature and expecting from her little except the bare necessities of existence. Shrugging their shoulders and gesturing vaguely towards the enormous heavens, they accepted with a fatalistic resignation not only physical hardship but also cruel social injustice and political repression. Occasionally their resentment flared up into rebellion and brutal violence, but more often they took refuge in bouts of drunken gaiety which passed only to leave them more gloomy and apathetic than before. Yet Gogol hints at the mysterious spell which the countryside wove over them. Beneath the great skies and through the bitter winters they clung with a fierce possessiveness to the soil of Mother Russia. Distrusting change and strangers, they huddled in close-knit communities and resisted progress. Against invaders they defended the homeland with a dogged and indestructible patriotism.

It would be wrong however to conclude that Russia had produced no bold and adventurous spirits. Indeed, her whole history was a record of ceaseless migration and settlement by a long succession of hunters, warriors, monks, and merchants. Among the most famous of these were the Cossacks of the western steppes, a freebooting brotherhood of adventurers, runaway serfs and fugitives from justice who acknowledged no authority except that of their elected leaders and lived by hunting, fishing, and plundering raids upon their wealthier neighbours. In the sixteenth century the Cossacks had spearheaded Russia's expansion across the Ural hills into the vast forests and marshes of Siberia. For centuries before that the peoples of the north had been at work, carving out settlements among the woods and forests around the headwaters of the river Volga. It would be equally wrong to conclude, as most of Europe did in the nineteenth century, that Russia was uncivilized. In the early middle ages the city of Kiev, on a bluff above the river Dnieper, had boasted Christian churches, palaces, schools, and libraries to rival those of Constantinople and the cities of the West. In the same period the merchants of Novgorod, situated among the forests of the north, had established a flourishing Baltic trade in furs and timbers. After this however the dark ages of Russia had begun. Barbarian invaders, the squat Asiatic Tatars, rode hunched in the saddles of their ponies across the steppes to burn and sack Kiev and the cities of the north. For two centuries they exacted tribute from southern and central Russia and reduced its budding civilization to a cultural wilderness of warriors and peasants. Novgorod escaped their domination only to meet the invasion of the Teutonic Knights, pressing eastwards across the Baltic plain.

2 A Russian landscape: great rivers, endless
plains, and enormous skies, dwarfing humanity
into insignificance

Calling themselves crusaders but as barbarous in their actions as the Tatars,
the Knights wrought havoc before a prince of Novgorod, Alexander
Nevsky, checked their advance in 1242 in a battle by the frozen lake of
Pskov which has been made famous by the Soviet cinema. Novgorod
survived, but her route to the Baltic was closed and much of her prosperity
disappeared.

When Russia emerged from her dark ages in the fifteenth century,
therefore, much of her early promise had been stifled and her isolation
from the West had begun. The Church remained as a civilizing influence,
but nothing illustrates more clearly than the history of the Russian Church
the effects of this isolation upon her life. The Church of Kiev was an off-
shoot of the eastern Church of Constantinople, which itself broke away
from Roman Christendom in the early middle ages and never effectively

3   Russian monks and priests. Their unprepossess-
ing appearance typifies the ignorance and backwardness of so much of Russia's religious life

healed the breach in the centuries which followed. In the thirteenth century the monks of Kiev fled for protection from the Tatars to the northern cities and eventually to Moscow. When Constantinople itself was captured by the Turks in 1453 the breach with the West became complete. The Russian Church declared that Moscow had become the third Rome, the authentic heir of historic Christendom which alone had preserved the purity of the faith. Its language, its rituals, its beliefs, and even its calendar became divorced from Western influences and Russia escaped all contact with the great religious and social upheaval of sixteenth-century Europe. The Russian reformation was confined to theological disputes, bitter enough in themselves, over such matters as the correct spelling of the name of Jesus or whether two fingers or three should be used to make the sign of the Cross. By the eighteenth century the Orthodox Church of Russia had become a byword for superstition and reaction in enlightened western Europe. Voltaire wrote:

> Their religion was and remains that of the Greek Christians, but mixed up with superstitions to which, the more extravagant and onerous they are, the more they are attached. Few Muscovites dare to eat pigeon, because the Holy Spirit is depicted in the form of a dove. They observe as a rule four Lents a year, and during these periods of abstinence they dare eat neither eggs nor milk. God and Saint Nicholas are the objects of their worship and, immediately after them, the Tsar and the Patriarch.

The Church, therefore, symbolized the isolation and the backwardness of Russia and also, in a superstitious and largely illiterate country, contributed powerfully to perpetuate this state of affairs. The Patriarch of Moscow was its spiritual head. The Tsar was the monarch who shared his prestige. Since the flight from Kiev an intimate partnership had existed between these two authorities. The Church repaid her protectors by exercising all her great influence to support and sanction the Russian monarchy as the representative of God on earth.

The men who disposed of this Divine Right in the nineteenth century were themselves the successors of warriors who had built their wooden fortress, or Kremlin, near the upper waters of the Volga in the twelfth century. Of all the Russians, these Muscovite princes had proved themselves to be the boldest, the most ambitious, and the most ruthless. Under the Tatars they had quickly established for themselves a privileged position as chief collectors of tribute from their neighbours. In later years they had played a more heroic role as liberators, driving the Tatars back to the

4   Repin's famous picture of the Cossacks, proud,
lawless, and freebooting, writing an insulting letter
to the Sultan of Turkey

Volga and the southern steppes. To these achievements they had added, later still, diplomacy. Ivan the Great (1462–1505) married Zöe, the niece of the last emperor of Constantinople, and took over to himself both the title of Tsar, which is a corruption of Caesar, and the double-headed eagle of Byzantium as his coat-of-arms. The price which Russia paid for her liberation from the Tatars was the establishment of the autocratic power of the Tsars. Novgorod and the other northern city-states fell to them in turn and Kiev escaped only because she fell into a new subjection to the Catholic kings of the great joint kingdom of Lithuania–Poland. During the sixteenth and seventeenth centuries Moscow and Poland fought for the lands which lay between them. At first the contest went in favour of the Poles and for a short time at the beginning of the seventeenth century a Polish prince sat on the throne of Moscow. He was expelled however and in his place the young prince Michael Romanov was elected as Tsar, founding the dynasty which was to rule Russia for the next 300 years. Under the Romanovs Kiev and the Ukraine were won back from the Poles and the Cossacks also became subjects of Moscow. Russia's open frontiers, which had made her so vulnerable to invasion in earlier centuries, presented an invitation to expansion under strong and energetic rulers. The Romanovs advanced west into the Baltic lands, east into Asia and finally, at the end of the eighteenth century, south into the steppes where this history began.

Over the whole of this expanding empire the Romanov heirs of Moscow established a royal authority which was the most absolute in Europe. In part it was the feudal authority of warrior-kings over their vassals, whom they rewarded with lands for their service and obedience. In part, however it was also the authority of Tatar khans over their tributaries and Byzantine autocrats over their Christian subjects. Finally, in the eighteenth century, Peter the Great (1682–1725) converted all these ancient sources of authority into a modern absolutism. Constantly at war to extend his frontiers, Peter made Russia into a military machine, designed to produce the men and materials he needed for his task. Taking Prussia and Scandinavia as his examples, he conscripted both landowners and peasants to compulsory military service. To this he added a poll-tax and numerous other taxes, including imposts on beards and baths. To collect his taxes and administer his wars he created a huge formal bureaucracy. Despising the Church for everything except her wealth, he made the Holy Synod a government department and converted that wealth to the use of the state. Peter the Great was succeeded by a series of weak rulers, most of them women, but the iron fetters of authority which he riveted upon Russia were never completely struck off and both the Tsars of the nineteenth century and the Communist rulers of the twentieth enjoyed his inheritance.

The experiences of some of Peter's eighteenth-century successors indicate however that, at least to some extent, the power of the Tsars derived from a bargain with their noblemen. Peter III (1762), in the short period before he was murdered by his palace guards, was obliged to release the nobility from their obligatory service to the state. His wife Catherine (1762–96), the German princess who succeeded him, added their exemption from personal taxation and confirmed their exclusive power over their serfs. Serfdom was the final and the most onerous burden which her rulers imposed upon Russia. It was a set of social customs, underwritten by the law, which made over half the peasant population virtually the chattels of their landlords. It was not unique to Russia and, indeed, it had not existed either in Kievan Russia or under the Tatar yoke, but in succeeding centuries it had developed over almost the whole of the empire and in the eighteenth, when it began finally to disappear elsewhere on the continent, the Tsars confirmed and extended it. The institution of serfdom derived basically from the landowners' insatiable demand for labour in the ever-increasing territories which Russia occupied. The peasants contributed by falling into debt. At first they had hired their labour to the landowners in return for some land of their own but, through custom and law, their labour-service became obligatory. The Tsars encouraged the process because grants of peasants, like gifts of estates, served to purchase the loyalty of the nobility. By making the peasants a subject population, it consolidated their own authority and made easier the conscription of soldiers and the collection of the poll-tax. Peter the Great declared that even the remaining free peasants were 'state peasants', liable to conscription and taxation like all the rest. With such labourers he built his new city of St Petersburg, condemning thousands of them to death from fever as they struggled to lay in the Baltic marshes the foundations of the great streets and palaces which were to make his city the equal of the capitals of the West.

By the beginning of the nineteenth century the power of landowners over their serfs had become absolute. 'Landowners do whatever seems good to them on their estates', wrote Catherine, 'except inflict capital punishment: that is forbidden'.

In addition to his economic power the landowner was prosecutor and judge in his own court. He could and did inflict savage punishments of flogging, torture, and imprisonment in chains. He was not, in practice, held responsible for a serf's death unless it occurred immediately after the punishment had been administered. He could sell the serf's land from under his feet, or sell the serfs without the land. He could split up families for the purposes of sale, and offer serfs for purchase in the market-place. Of course, not every landowner was a sadistic tyrant. Many were benevolent men and even those interested only in the profitability of their estates appreciated that contented peasants were more likely to work well for them than slaves driven to their labours by the lash. For all practical purposes however the Russian serfs were slaves as truly as the Blacks who toiled upon the plantations of the southern states of America. To borrow the phrase of the American south, serfdom was also Russia's 'peculiar institution'. Neither the Tsar nor the landowners could imagine a life without it. Or perhaps they could, but feared what they imagined. Towards the end of the eighteenth century a great rising of serfs occurred in the area between the Volga and

5   Catherine the Great, the German princess who, after the assassination of her husband, became one of Russia's greatest rulers, famous for her learning, her lovers, and her territorial conquests

6 Pugachov's rebels put a noble family on trial

the Urals. A rumour spread that Peter III had intended to liberate the serfs at the same time that he released the nobles from their obligations. An illiterate Cossack, Emilian Pugachov, claimed to be Peter III and called upon serfs to rise and liberate themselves. For more than a year, from 1772–4, he exercised a reign of terror in the captured city of Kazan and threatened to march on Moscow itself. Three thousand men, women, and children, most of them members of the landowning class, were put to death before an army was recalled from the war with Turkey to suppress the rebellion. Pugachov went to Moscow in a cage and was publicly beheaded and quartered. His death was a dreadful example to serfs but his career terrified more than a generation of noblemen and served perhaps more than any argument to discredit suggestions of reform.

There can be no doubt, however, of the demoralizing and retarding effect which the institution of serfdom exercised upon Russian society. Quite apart from its inherent cruelty and injustice, it produced a rural population which was idle, ignorant, and cunning rather than hardworking, enterprising, and self-confident. In the same way serfdom demoralized the masters. Members of a leisure class dependent for everything upon the services of others, they lost the ability to think and act for themselves. With few exceptions, they lost interest even in the efficient exploitation of their estates, and passed away their lives in a stupefying boredom which echoes through the pages of every novel and play of upper-class Russian life in the nineteenth century. Their ignorance and apathy was reflected in the sphere of politics, where tsardom also intervened to deprive them of any ambition except to protect their privileges. Their only aim, if they could bring themselves to abandon the bucolic pleasures of country life, was to serve the monarch as officers or bureaucrats. It was unnecessary for the Tsars to make such service obligatory. As soldiers, the Russian nobles showed themselves heroically brave but hopelessly incompetent. As administrators they were equally inept and also corrupt. Of all the factors which contributed to make Russia the primitive and backward land which Gogol described in the passage with which this chapter opened, tsardom and serfdom were the most crucially important. No doubt

7 Serfdom: a nineteenth-century engraving illustrates the debasement which the institution brought to both serfs and the nobles who were their masters

the climate and the landscape contributed also. It is also true, as many historians have stressed, that Russia was a huge country in which it was difficult to construct the communications without which progress could not spread. So was North America, however, but size and natural obstacles did not prevent its rapid development in the nineteenth century. Only in the southern states did America stand still, and this was because of the stultifying effects of slavery. In Russia also the political and social institutions which had developed from her history were the chief barriers to change.

Thus, when the nineteenth century opened, Russia also was standing still while Europe moved. While western Europe abandoned the archaic system of communal farming, with its widely-scattered holdings and wasteful fallows, Russia perpetuated these obsolescent methods and imported them unchanged into the virgin soil of the steppes. While western Europe launched into industrial revolution, the Russian merchants clung jealously to their guild-privileges and the Jews, the only business-minded section of the minute town-dwelling population, were a hated minority restricted to living in certain areas and practising a limited range of trades. The towns themselves remained huddled collections of wooden buildings around unpaved streets and Russia gave the disease of cholera to Europe. Only the shining cupolas of churches and monasteries rose above the depressing skyline, symbols of the power which the Church retained and employed to stifle education and free enquiry. Few Russians travelled outside their country before the Napoleonic War, and those who did were liable to imprisonment or even execution if they spread the ideas of the West upon their return. While the theories of democracy began to undermine the fabric of absolute monarchy elsewhere, the Russian nobles rejected even the few schemes laid before them which would have established representative institutions in Russia. Russia remained isolated from Europe and, within Russia, the nobility remained isolated from the people. The nobles of the court lived in the splendid palaces of St Petersburg, wore the elegant fashions of France, and spoke French in preference to their native tongue, which they regarded as a barbarous jargon fit only for the use of the peasants. The peasants themselves lived in smoke-filled, one-roomed cabins, dressed in smocks, sheepskins, and shoes made of tree-bark, and accepted their lot as the will of God and the Tsar.

Could anyone recognize the state of Russia and, having recognized, transform it? Ironically, only the Tsars themselves had sufficient power to do so. Peter the Great had been the first to recognize how pitifully his country compared with the West and had made strenuous efforts to encourage industry, technical education, and the arts, even cutting off beards and practising dentistry himself upon the reluctant members of his court. Because he had relied entirely upon his own powers, however, most of his reforms had died with him, leaving only the power behind. The case of Catherine had been different. Although known to history chiefly for her succession of lovers, Catherine was an intelligent and cultured woman who planned to give Russia a codified legal system and to reform the conditions of serfdom. The circumstances in which she came to the throne did not allow her to risk the opposition of the nobility, however, and her reforms remained nothing but paper schemes. This was the irony of tsardom; just because its power had become so great as a result of the existing system, the Tsars stood to lose most from the effects of change. Only by maintaining Russia's backwardness, in short, did they know how to rule her. A cruel dilemma therefore confronted the nineteenth-century successors of Peter and Catherine. Almost without exception they recognized the need for change but reached similar conclusions with regard to its implementation. The problems were too great, the risks too frightening, and the time not yet ripe to take the necessary steps. Alexander I (1801–25) postponed and finally evaded the solution of his problems. Nicholas I (1825–55) took a perverse pride in Russia's backwardness and tried to preserve it without contamination by the West. Alexander II (1855–81) abolished serfdom but was himself hounded by assassins until they struck him down. Alexander III (1881–94) attempted to combine economic change with the retention of his autocratic power. Nicholas II (1894–1917) rowed stubbornly and uncomprehendingly against the tide of history until it engulfed him. None of these men could be called successful. The grim fatalism of which nature made men so conscious in Russia seemed to hold in its unrelenting grip even the highest rulers of the unhappy land.

One final consideration distracted the attention of Russia's rulers from their problems and contributed to their fate. True heirs to the Muscovite tradition, they were obsessed by the ambition to extend their territories beyond the limits so far reached. With few exceptions, however, they were less successful than their predecessors and encountered a series of diplomatic humiliations and military defeats. These foreign conflicts played a decisive part in Russian history. They revealed and emphasized to a growing number of people within Russia the gap which existed between Russia and

17

the great powers with whom she competed, and thus strengthened a slowly growing demand for change at home. The defeats also weakened the historic prestige of the Tsars. A second gap appeared, therefore, between the Tsars and their people. At first no more than a crack in the surface of loyalty, it widened and deepened as time went on to become finally a chasm. Eventually the strain upon the ancient ties of loyalty became too great and they parted, leaving tsardom to fall into the abyss. More than a century passed before this happened, however. The seeds of revolution took as long to

8 The Nevsky Prospect: the most famous avenue
of fashionable St Petersburg, and the background
for innumerable scenes in Russian novels

flower as did the bloom of tsardom to wither and to die. The interim is a
fascinating story of missed opportunities and hopes betrayed. Since it is
also a story of good intentions frustrated by blind opposition, fruitless
violence and perhaps by an inexorable fate, it contains the essential elements
of tragedy.

2 Alexander and Napoleon

THE FIRST TSAR to rule Russia in the nineteenth century was Paul (1796–1801). He was the son of Catherine but had been taken away from his mother at birth and no affection existed between them. Instead Catherine regarded her son as an unpleasant reminder of her husband's death and a possible focus for similar plots against herself. She also regarded him as a fool and freely voiced the opinion that he was unfit to rule. Deliberately kept at a distance from the court, Paul filled his time by drilling soldiers to the point of exhaustion upon his country estate and brooding over his father's death and his own neglect. He became a moody tyrant who, when he finally succeeded to the throne against his late mother's will, filled the prisons with men whom he suspected of disloyalty. He made a determined attempt to re-assert the full power of the Tsar over the nobility and rapidly became unpopular. Finally he involved Russia, upon the slightest of pretexts, in fruitless wars with both France and England. When he ordered the Cossacks to march on India in 1801 his courtiers took this as conclusive evidence that he was mad. He was deposed and strangled, to be succeeded by his eldest son Alexander.

Alexander was almost certainly implicated in the plot against his father although probably he had not expected it to end as it did. This grisly outcome may have weighed upon his conscience in later years for he was a sensitive man. It was not held against him by anyone at the time however. The new Tsar seemed everything that his father had not been. He was young, good-looking, charming, and agreeable to everyone he met. As time went by he was to prove as unpredictable as his father, but at his accession St Petersburg was filled with relief and hope. Catherine had intended that her eldest grandson should succeed her and carry through the reforms which she had failed to achieve. To this end his education had been entrusted to a Swiss tutor, César Laharpe, who was a man of radical and even republican views. The new Tsar's friends were young liberal noblemen who also encouraged him to come to grips with the twin problems of serfdom

9 Paul I: a cruel, post-humous caricature gives the popular view of an unpopular Tsar

and absolutism. Alexander himself spoke bitterly of 'the state of barbarism to which the country has been reduced by the traffic in men', although with an early premonition of the pessimism which was later to overwhelm him he remarked, on another occasion, that to reform Russia was a task 'impossible not only for a man of ordinary powers, like myself, but even for a genius'. His wide blue eyes and his simple, open features bespoke Alexander's transparently good intentions but also indicated, perhaps, a certain detachment from the unpleasant business of reality and a lack of the will to persist and succeed. The first evidence of this appeared with his law on serfdom of 1803. His 'unofficial committee' of liberal friends had urged him to begin the emancipation of the serfs, arguing that the country landowners were too politically ignorant and too accustomed to obedience to mount effective resistance. Remembering his father's death, Alexander was more cautious. His law confined itself to permitting landowners to free their serfs provided that they gave them land as well. Not surprisingly, this altered little. By the end of the reign no more than a few thousand serfs had benefited from the measure and their numbers were more than balanced

by those of the free peasants whom Alexander had made over to private serfdom.

The failure to attack serfdom was the first disappointment of Alexander's reign and the committee of friends dissolved soon afterwards, although some of its members were to retain their influence in later years. At first however they were succeeded by a remarkable individual, Michael Speransky, the son of a village priest who rose from being a teacher of mathematics to become for a few years the closest adviser of the Tsar. Speransky was a reserved and lonely man whose pale, bespectacled face and lack of social graces made him few friends at court, while his ideas won him many powerful enemies. At Alexander's suggestion Speransky took up Catherine's scheme for a codification of the Russian legal system. His methodical mind expanded this into a draft which would have given Russia a constitution similar in many ways to that of Britain or the U.S.A. He proposed a separation of the executive, legislative, and judicial powers. Although the Tsar would retain his ultimate control, Speransky proposed nothing less than the creation of a Russian parliament, or Duma, an elected body with power to veto the Tsar's laws and to introduce legislation of its own. What might have happened to Russia and her Tsars in the next century, had this scheme been adopted, is the first of the imponderable questions of Russian history in this period. As a constitutional monarchy, tsardom might have developed and survived while Russia drew the accruing benefits. None of this happened however. Speransky's noble enemies increased their pressure for his removal and on an evening in 1812 he was called to an interview in his master's study. He emerged with a rare show of emotion, in tears. Alexander had dismissed him and sent him to govern eastern Siberia. The Tsar himself complained next day that 'They have taken Speransky away from me, and he was my right arm'. In doing so the Russian nobility had revealed the political ignorance of which they had been accused. They were now left once again at the mercy of a Tsar's whims. The first result of this was to involve the country in a foreign policy which led to the invasion and devastation of Russia.

At the beginning of the nineteenth century Europe was dominated by the figure of Napoleon Bonaparte, the brilliant general who transformed a

11   Reserved and lonely, Michael Speransky was however the one man who could have made tsardom a constitutional monarchy and perhaps averted its ultimate collapse

23

desperate war for the defence of the French republic into a series of campaigns for the extension of his personal empire. He fascinated and terrified the continent by turns. Some nobles at St Petersburg admired him just as they admired everything French and despised all that was Russian. They regarded him as Russia's natural ally on the road of progress. Both Paul and Alexander saw him in a different light however. To them the French usurper appeared as a threat to the cause of monarchy everywhere. Alexander, perhaps, had a more personal motive for his dislike. In 1804 the agents of the French emperor had kidnapped a prince of the former royal house of Bourbon from his refuge outside France and executed him for plotting against the new régime. When the Tsar protested Napoleon coolly enquired why so little progress had been made in apprehending and punishing the assassins of his father Paul.

Whether from policy or pique, in 1805 Alexander formed a coalition with Britain and the Holy Roman Emperor against Napoleon. The sequel was disastrous. Thwarted by the fleet in his attempt to invade England, Napoleon marched east across Europe and smashed the joint armies of Austria and Russia on a snow-covered hillside at Austerlitz, a village 100 miles north of Vienna. The battle marked the end of the Holy Roman Empire and Alexander himself fled with his shattered army from the field. Soon afterwards William Pitt, the British Prime Minister, died and his country's war effort was temporarily interrupted. For a few months the Tsar found a new ally in the King of Prussia but before the end of 1806 Napoleon defeated the Prussians at Jena and occupied Berlin. He continued to march east and for almost another year the Russians fought on alone. Napoleon was held in another winter battle at Eylau, in East Prussia, at the beginning of 1807 but then inflicted another smashing defeat at Friedland. Ruined harvests and the interruption of British subsidies had made Russia's internal position desperate also and Alexander had no alternative to seeking an armistice. On a barge moored in the river Niemen at the very frontier of Russia, the Tsar and the Emperor met and embraced as brothers. They met again, with even more splendid ceremonial, at Erfurt a year later. Napoleon asked for the hand of a Russian princess in marriage. None of this outward show could conceal Russia's weakness, however, and Napoleon drove a hard bargain. At the end of the eighteenth century, during Catherine's reign, Russia, Austria, and Prussia had partitioned the weakened kingdom of Poland among themselves. Alexander was now allowed to annexe the last part of eastern Poland which had eluded his

ARCTIC OCEAN

miles 500

URAL MOUNTAINS

S W E D E N

F I N L A N D

GULF OF FINLAND

St.Petersburg

Vyatka

Novgorod

Volga

Kazan

Pskov

Nizhni
Novgorod

Dvina

Moscow

Borodino

Orenburg

Niemen

Smolensk

Tilsit

Kirgiz

B A L T I C   S E A

Warsaw

Pripet

P O L A N D

ARAL
SEA

Galicia

Kiev

Ukraine

Dnieper

Donetz

Volga

Khiva

Bug

Dniester

Astrakhan

Moldavia

Don

Azov

Wallachia

Kuban

Crimea

Circassia

C
A
S
P
I
A
N

Derbent

Daghestan

Danube

Sebastopol

B L A C K   S E A

Tiflis

Georgia

S
E
A

Bulgaria

Armenia

O T T O M A N   E M P I R E

Constantinople

P E R S I A

The Straits

MAP NO. I
European Russia at the beginning of the nineteenth century

25

12 The Tilsit alliance: The Tsar and Emperor
meet as brothers on a barge moored in the river
Niemen: but Napoleon drove a hard bargain which
proved impossible for Alexander to fulfil

grandmother, but Napoleon took the rest and renamed it the Grand Duchy
of Warsaw. He agreed to allow Alexander a free hand in the Turkish empire
and also to the Russian annexation of Finland from Sweden. In return
however Russia agreed to adhere to the Continental System, the great
scheme for the control of European commerce by which Napoleon hoped
to close the continent to British trade and bring his western enemy to
bankruptcy.

In fact it was Russia which came nearest to bankruptcy in the years
which followed. Exports of timber, iron ore, and flax to England slumped
disastrously and an adverse trade balance brought a spiral of inflation which
robbed the rouble of four-fifths of its value. Not even the ingenuity of
Speransky could stave off a catastrophic economic depression. Meanwhile
Napoleon strengthened his grip on central Europe, threatening to invade
Prussia once again and reviving in Poland nationalist hopes that, with his
assistance, the Lithuanian territories might be won back from Russia.

The Tilsit alliance brought nothing but evil consequences to Russia and, when the marriage negotiations were delayed, Napoleon added a final insult by marrying an Austrian princess. Finally the Tsar's ambassador insisted that the commercial and territorial demands must be relaxed. In reply, late in June 1812, Napoleon launched his Grand Army across the Niemen and invaded Russia.

It is difficult to decide which of the two emperors had taken the more reckless decision. Napoleon had undertaken to conquer a vast country which was certain to be stubbornly defended. His army numbered 600,000 men however and they were superbly confident. Victors of Austerlitz and Friedland and conquerors of Vienna, Berlin, Rome, and Madrid, they expected Moscow and St Petersburg to fall in their turn. The Lithuanian landowners greeted them as liberators and the sullen peasants in the Russian villages through which Napoleon passed seemed to him no better than savages. In fact both the Tsar and his people were determined to resist but the generals understandably feared a massive confrontation with the conqueror of Europe which might lead to a renewed defeat and the collapse of the motherland. They narrowly escaped such a defeat at Smolensk and resolved thereafter on a more evasive strategy. As the Grand Army advanced slowly through a hot, dry summer the Russians withdrew before them, burning villages and crops as they went. Not until they reached Borodino, a hillside village less than 100 miles from Moscow itself, were they prepared to make a stand and there, in the first week of September, invaders and defenders engaged in a conflict which Napoleon described as 'the most terrible of all my battles'. He watched the battle through a telescope and, when it was over, his horse could hardly make its way through the piled bodies of the fallen. The French counted 30,000 casualties and the Russians 40,000.

After this the Russians retreated again and within a few days Napoleon stood in sight of the citadel of the Tsars. One of his officers wrote later,

Seen from the top of that last hill, Moscow had an oriental or, rather, an enchanted appearance, with its five hundred domes either gilded or painted in the gaudiest colours and standing out here and there above a veritable sea of houses. It was a magnificent sight. Nevertheless, I noticed many anxious expressions among the French officers. There was surprise at seeing no deputation come out. 'They will wait a long time,' said a veteran of our regiment, 'All those Russians will emigrate to Siberia rather than surrender'.

27

13 Napoleon's first sight of Moscow: 'seen from
the top of that last hill, Moscow had an oriental,
or rather an enchanted appearance'

The city had been evacuated by all but its poorest inhabitants. The army
had marched east and then turned sharply south so that the French temporarily lost contact with it. The Tsar and his court had gone to St Petersburg, where Alexander paced the grounds of his residence in solitary gloom.
When he appeared on the cathedral steps on the anniversary of his accession he was greeted with stony silence by his people. Napoleon met a
similar welcome in Moscow. His quarters were prepared in the Kremlin
and from its windows, on the first night of the occupation, flames could be
seen in the suburbs. Whether these fires were started by French looters or
on the orders of the Russian governor as he left, remains uncertain.
Within a few days however the wind had raised a conflagration which
destroyed the wooden houses of the city. The French were driven into the
stone structures which remained and Napoleon's horses were stabled in a
cathedral.

A ruined city without its Tsar was a fruitless conquest. French envoys
set out for St Petersburg and also to make contact with the Russian army

14 Napoleon watches from the Kremlin while
Moscow burns

to the south. The Tsar had forbidden all communication with the enemy
however and Napoleon was faced with the necessity for a critical decision.
He wished to march on St Petersburg but his marshals demurred. They
knew the poor condition of their men and were also becoming fearful of
the approaching Russian winter. Moscow itself, on the other hand, was
becoming a trap as the Russians closed in. Always impatient and knowing
that western Europe was becoming restless in his absence, the Emperor
decided to retreat to Smolensk and immediately began the withdrawal. As
his army retreated regular units of the Russian army emerged to bar the
way and were beaten off only at heavy cost. Partisan guerrillas made
sudden marauding attacks upon the baggage-trains and long lines of
stragglers. They left few survivors and these the peasants captured and
tortured, often burying them alive. The French were reduced to killing
and eating their transport horses for want of food and, when they reached
Smolensk, discovered that the garrison which had been left there had eaten
most of its supplies. The desperate soldiers looted what was left within a

day of their arrival and it was clearly out of the question to stay the winter in Smolensk. The retreat recommenced.

The Grand Army now numbered less than half the men who had left Moscow. As it approached the river Berezina Russian armies closed in from north, east, and south and only by a prodigious effort was Napoleon able to get his advance-guard across the river by pontoon bridges. After this he abandoned the rest of his army and pressed on into Europe. He left orders for the bridges to be destroyed and a dreadful panic ensued as stragglers and camp-followers scrambled to get across in time to escape the pursuing Cossacks. Many fell into the freezing river and many more were left behind to be slaughtered. For those who succeeded in crossing there were conditions as bad or worse to come. The winter set in, some weeks earlier than usual, and the Russians abandoned pursuit and left the climate to do their work for them. Transport waggons had to be abandoned on the icy roads and men who fell by the way were stripped of their uniforms by their numbed and demoralized comrades. The Grand Army disintegrated. At the end of the year less than 5,000 men recrossed the Niemen as an organized military force and during the next few months no more than 100,000 altogether emerged from the country which they had entered so proudly only six months before. Russia had been liberated and, although the cost had been terrible, the Tsar's prestige was restored.

Alexander's volatile spirits now recovered and, against the advice of his generals, he pursued Napoleon into Europe. A new coalition was formed and in 1813 a Russian army took part in the battle of Leipzig which freed Germany from French control. In 1814 Alexander rode into Paris beside the King of Prussia as one of the liberators of Europe. Russian troops were absent from the final campaign of 1815 which led to Napoleon's defeat at Waterloo but Alexander played a full part in the sessions of the Congress of Vienna which met to decide the future of Europe. It was the first time in living memory that a Russian ruler had visited the West and the Tsar's handsome appearance and mild manners made a good impression. It seemed hard to link this sophisticated and amiable man with his savage and backward country and a French diplomat concluded that Alexander was 'the civilized ruler of an uncivilized people'. Even more difficult to understand were the motives of the eastern autocrat who now proposed that Europe's frontiers should be decided by national boundaries rather than by dynastic claims. It was largely in order to prevent such an unwelcome development that the wars with Napoleon had been fought and, in any

30

case, it was well-known that behind the scenes Russia was intriguing with Prussia to recover the whole of Poland for herself. And what were Europe's statesmen to make of Alexander's final proposal to create a Holy Alliance of sovereigns

> taking for their sole guide the precepts of Religion, namely the precepts of Justice, Christian Charity, and Peace, which, far from being applicable only to private concerns, must guide all their steps, as being the only means of consolidating human institutions and remedying their imperfections?

Cynical diplomats concluded that the Tsar was a fool. The British foreign secretary described the scheme as 'a piece of sublime mysticism and nonsense' and refused to have anything to do with it. Prince Metternich of Austria thought that 'the Tsar's mind was quite clearly affected'. The Holy Alliance was concluded among all the powers except Britain, but only to become an international organization for the suppression of nationalist

15 The retreat from Moscow: the remnants of the Grand Army and their camp-followers struggle across the river Berezina while winter and the watching Russians close in

16 Servile and ingratiating towards the Tsar, but
a sadistic monster to everyone within his power,
Arakcheyev dominated the last years of the reign
of Alexander I and was blamed for everything that
happened, or failed to happen, then

and democratic ideas, apparently almost the opposite of what Alexander had intended.

What did the Tsar intend, however, and how clearly did he understand his own intentions? These questions are bound to arise in any consideration of Alexander's career, because his words and actions were so often inconsistent. A puzzle to posterity, he was a man of mystery to his contemporaries also. While Europe found it hard to plumb his diplomatic motives, his countrymen were equally perplexed by his decisions nearer home. Having acquired Poland, Alexander, perhaps at the suggestion of the Polish prince Adam Czartoryski, a survivor of the earlier committee of friends, granted a parliamentary constitution and sanctioned the formation of a Polish national army. Reactionaries thought that the Tsar was sowing dragon's teeth and, as so often happened in Russian history, events in the next reign proved them right. Reformers hoped that Poland was perhaps the laboratory for Russia. At the same period serfs were freed in the Baltic lands. Was this also an experiment which might be repeated, if successful, in Russia herself? In fact the experiment was not successful, because the Baltic serfs were freed without land and became a miserable and rebellious lower class. No further moves were made to end serfdom in Russia and no parliament was created in Moscow or St Petersburg to match that which met in Warsaw. Instead, as the years went by, Alexander became increasingly religious and increasingly conservative, and correspondingly more distrustful of liberal ideas. Young men who shared his earlier enthusiasm for change now found themselves subjected to renewed censorship and police activity.

Traditionally loyal to their Tsar and still, to some extent, bewitched by his gentle charm, most Russians hesitated to reproach Alexander himself for what had happened or failed to happen in the second half of his reign. Instead they laid the blame upon his new chief adviser, Alexis Arakcheyev. Arakcheyev was a soldier and a confidant of Alexander's father, a fact which perhaps goes some way to explain the ascendancy which he now established over the uneasy conscience of the Tsar. His personality made him an ideal target for universal hatred. Towards the Tsar he was fawning and servile but to the nobles and to his fellow-ministers he was arrogant and overbearing. Towards those completely within his power, such as the soldiers of his regiment and the serfs on his estates, he was a sadistic monster. He gathered all the separate reins of government into his own hands in the years after the great war of liberation, and Alexander was gratefully ready to have him do so. When the Tsar wished to have a paper on serfdom, Arakcheyev prepared it. When a mutinous regiment had to be suppressed he was equally willing to oblige.

The philosopher Tolstoy wrote half a century later:

> In the mechanism of the state organism, these men are as necessary as wolves in the organism of nature. . . . It is only on the theory of this necessity that one can explain the fact that a man so cruel – capable of pulling out grenadiers' moustaches with his own hand – though unable, from the weakness of his nerves, to face danger, so uncultured, so boorish, as Arakcheyev, was able to retain such influence with a sovereign of such chivalrous tenderness and nobility of character like Alexander.

Arakcheyev, therefore, was Alexander's alibi in the last years of his reign. The Tsar himself had done nothing to change the face of Russia. He had liberated the motherland from the invader, however, and this was sufficient to make him venerated as 'Alexander the Blessed' when he died in 1825. Even his death remains shrouded in an aura of mystery however, for a rumour at once became current that he had not died (he was still aged less than fifty) but retired to live the life of a pious hermit in the countryside. If by any chance true, this story is a fitting conclusion to the reign of a Tsar who had neither ignored the existence of his problems nor faced up to them, but increasingly evaded them by retreat into a private world.

Nor had everyone in Russia forgiven the Tsar for the disappointments which he had inflicted upon his country. The war of liberation and the Polish experiment had raised the hopes of some members of the young Russian generation and when the Tsar failed them they began to discuss means of forcing the pace of change themselves. Such a young man was Paul Pestel, a cavalry officer wounded at Borodino at the age of nineteen and since then much travelled in Europe and deeply read in her political philosophy. Pestel became a member of the Union of Salvation, a society dedicated to the reform of Russia. Despatched to serve in the distant military province of Bessarabia, he occupied his time in developing wide-ranging ideas for the future of the country. Arakcheyev must go but so also must the Tsar. In his place must be created a republic ruled by a revolutionary dictatorship. The nobility must be destroyed and the land either nationalized or redistributed to enterprising peasants. These were remarkably radical ideas – the beginning in fact of the Russian Socialist tradition which was to culminate in the Bolshevik dictatorship of 1917 and the establishment of Communism in Russia. They were far ahead of their time, as Pestel discovered when he travelled to St Petersburg to put his scheme before members of the society there. Ideas which seemed capable of realization when brooded over in Bessarabia became wild and dangerous in the city where Arakcheyev ruled. Indeed the police were well aware of the society's clandestine meetings but Alexander characteristically refused to have the young noblemen arrested.

In 1825 his reign ended, however, and the revolutionary moment, such as it was, occurred. Alexander had left the succession as confused as every other aspect of his reign. He had no son and his brother Constantine was

17 Colonel Paul Pestel: military man and radical revolutionary

heir-apparent. Constantine had lived for years in Poland and contracted
an unsuitable marriage. In 1822 he had announced his intention of renounc-
ing his claim in favour of a third brother, Nicholas. In December 1825 he
would neither confirm his decision nor come to St Petersburg. Nicholas,
sensing the restlessness among the officers of the garrison, resolved to act
and had himself proclaimed Tsar. The reforming officers raised a cry of
'Constantine and the Constitution'. In a day of confusion in the streets
of the capital 3,000 soldiers went over to them, although many seemed
hardly to understand what they were doing and thought that 'Constitution'
was Constantine's wife. Nine thousand of the garrison refused to move.
Nicholas appealed to the rebels to disperse and, when this failed, ordered
the streets to be cleared by cannon-fire. The rebels fled. A brief attempt by

18 The Decembrist mutiny. A day of confusion
in the streets and squares of St Petersburg before
Nicholas ordered them to be cleared by artillery-fire

the southern arm of the society to take Kiev ended in similar failure and the
'Men of December' were arrested. Pestel and four others were executed
and many were sent into exile. In itself, therefore, the Decembrist conspiracy was no more than a flash in the pan. The leaders had no following
and hardly a plan of what they hoped to achieve. Nevertheless, and viewed
through the perspective of what followed later, the December rising was a
starting-point. The revolutionary movement had begun, to run on a con-
verging course with tsardom for the next hundred years, even though the
immediate sequel was to impose thirty years of deliberate reaction upon
the Russian mind.

Николай Павловичъ.

Nicholas 1st

Emperor of all the Russias.

Александръ Николаевичъ.

GRAND DUKE ALEXANDER

Heir to the Throne?

Александра Феодоровна.

ALEXANDRA

Empress of all the Russias.

19   Nicholas I, his wife Alexandra, and the young
Grand Duke Alexander, later to become Alexander
II. A narrow-minded military autocrat, Nicholas
was also a conscientious ruler according to his
lights and determined to give his heir a broader
apprenticeship for tsardom than he had enjoyed
himself

3 Nicholas and the West

NICHOLAS I, who now ruled Russia for thirty years (1825–55), was brought up to be a soldier, not a Tsar. He looked upon the empire to which he had so unexpectedly succeeded as a military command. Disciplined obedience was the rule of his life: he expected it from all his subjects and dedicated himself to the office of monarchy. Every day he worked for long hours at government papers in his study, with a bust of Peter the Great on the desk before him. Nicholas admired his famous ancestor as a soldier and an autocrat however rather than as a reformer. Unlike Peter and unlike his own brother, Alexander, whose sophisticated education he had not shared, the new Tsar regarded western Europe as a Godless, democratic, anarchy. Russia had nothing to learn from the West, he believed. Rather it was his duty to preserve her from its baleful influence.

Orthodoxy, Autocracy, Nationality

became the official motto of the new reign. The Church enjoyed new power and influence and a determined attempt was made to convert Catholic, Protestant, Moslem, and Jewish subjects of the empire to the faith. The syllabuses of universities were purged of Western influences and remodelled upon a basis of the study of Russian language, history, and culture. The free discussion of ideas was more heavily censored than before.

This policy was a complete reversal of the general trend of the previous reign. There is no doubt that it was welcomed with a good deal of gruff approval by a great majority of the older generation. Among younger men and particularly students there was bound to be considerable opposition and to counter this Nicholas erected in Russia what may be called the first police-state in Europe. Its centre lay in the Third Department of the central government, an institution which developed such enormous power that it became virtually a secret government in itself. The agents of the Third Department were charged with spying and reporting upon all the other departments of the central administration and also sent confidential reports to the Tsar on the state of government in the provinces. They tracked political suspects, subversive intellectuals, religious schismatics, and foreign visitors to Russia. They shared with the religious authorities the censorship of literature and the theatre. The Department ran its own prisons, both in the capital and in Siberia, to which its victims were consigned without an open trial. Characteristically, the heavily paternalistic Nicholas regarded the Third Department as a benevolent institution, through which 'the voice of each citizen can reach the throne of the Tsar'. To its victims however it was an apparatus of terror. Among the most famous of these was the novelist Fedor Dostoevsky, who wrote an autobiographical account of his encounter with it in his *Notes from the House of the Dead*. As an educated and fervent young man of eighteen he had joined in the underground political discussions of St Petersburg. He was arrested with his colleagues, charged with 'impudent' criticism of Church and State and imprisoned for eight months in the grim fortress of Saints Peter and Paul. On a freezing December morning the political prisoners were led out to the execution yard and stripped to their shirts to stand shivering while sentence of death was pronounced. Three were tied to stakes and blindfolded and a firing-squad took aim. At the last moment however the officer in charge waved his handkerchief to stay the execution. 'At the Tsar's merciful behest', he announced, the sentence had been commuted to hard labour in Siberia. The three men were unbound. The hair of one of them had gone white, Dostoevsky recorded. Another had gone mad. The novelist himself was loaded with chains and began the journey to Siberia on Christmas Eve. For the next few years he felled trees at the penal settlement, sharing filthy quarters with murderers whose nostrils had been torn out by the public executioner and criminals who had been branded upon the forehead. At night the prisoners slept in chains and were flogged if they moaned too loudly in their sleep or did not sleep on the right side. Dostoevsky's permitted reading was restricted to the New Testament in Russian. His health, never strong, was ruined.

This was how Russia was ruled, at least in part, under the thirty years' reaction of Nicholas I. As was the case with so many repressive régimes in history, the system worked. The years of Nicholas's reign were a period of revolution in western and central Europe, when monarchs everywhere either fled from their palaces or granted the revolutionaries' demands while mobs stormed at their gates. No revolution occurred in Holy Russia however, although a Polish rising, led by Czartoryski and the army, flared up in 1830 and deposed Constantine. The rising was suppressed, however, as

20   As a fervent young student, the great novelist
Fedor Dostoevsky fell foul of the Third Department
and endured sufferings which ruined his fragile health

21 The grim fortress of Saints Peter and Paul,
Russia's great political prison throughout the
nineteenth century

was a second forlorn hope sixteen years later. In 1848 and 1849, the climactic years of European revolution, Nicholas was able to despatch his loyal troops to Hungary to help restore the authority of his neighbour and partner in the Holy Alliance, the Emperor of Austria. Not content with being the policeman of his own empire, Nicholas became known as 'the Gendarme of Europe', a title which he accepted with equanimity and some pride.

Apart from his ceaseless struggle with the forces of liberalism and democracy, a second obsession dominated the Tsar's career. This was 'the Greek project', as his grandmother Catherine had termed it, or 'the Eastern Question', as it appeared to western Europe. The object of these interests was the Turkish or Ottoman Empire, created in Europe's middle ages and extending from western Asia to the Danube and into northern Africa. The Turks had been great conquerors, spurred on by the conviction that, in invading Christian Europe, they were engaged in a Muslim Holy War. In 1453, as has been seen, they captured Constantinople and converted its great churches into mosques. In 1681 they had stood at the gates of Vienna. Since then however the Turkish Empire had entered its decline. It was Nicholas who coined for it in the nineteenth century the famous description of 'the Sick Man of Europe'. While the Christian peoples of south-eastern

Europe, the Serbs, the Greeks, the Roumanians, and the Bulgars, experienced a wave of nationalist excitement and made repeated bids to win their independence, the Sultans lost their vigour and idled in their golden palaces on the Bosphorus, relying upon their Muslim vassals, men such as Mohammed Ali, the Pasha of Egypt, to keep their empire for them.

Russia's interest in the affairs of this ramshackle empire derived from a variety of motives, the overriding and ultimate aim of which was to annexe Constantinople. This had been the purpose of Catherine's Greek project and her second grandson Constantine was significantly named, for he had been intended to restore to the city on the Bosphorus the Christian monarchy whose inheritance the Tsars of Russia claimed. The project had not been realized, and Constantine had gone to Poland. In the course of her long wars with Turkey, however, Catherine had succeeded in establishing for her heirs the right to protect the Christian subjects of the Sultan against injustice and oppression. Religious feeling was thus a basic motive in Russia's policy towards the Turks and there can be no doubt of its significance to Nicholas, who was devoutly Orthodox. Along with this idealistic motive however, and possibly cloaked by it to some extent, went more materialist aims. Constantinople stood on the Straits which led to the Black Sea and the Mediterranean. This seaway opened up a vulnerable cleft in Russian defences against the west, which Napoleon for one had planned to exploit before the treaty of Tilsit made him the ally of the Tsar. Russia wished to occupy Constantinople for reasons of national security. In the nineteenth century, moreover, the Straits acquired a new significance. As the steppes of southern Russia were opened to the plough, grain became an increasingly important export, and the Straits became a commercial artery of the national economy. The need to secure them became even more pressing.

Russia's motives towards the Turkish Empire, therefore, like those of all the imperialist powers of the nineteenth century, were a mixture of the sacred and the profane. Understandably, however, she could expect little sympathy for them from the West. Britain, in particular, feared that a Russian occupation of the Straits would imperil her own naval position in the Mediterranean, and the vision of Russian warships there became a recurrent nightmare of her statesmen. France shared this fear and Austria dreaded a Russian presence at the mouth of the Danube. The general policy of the West therefore became to block the Russian advance. Her statesmen set themselves the ultimately impossible task of preserving the Turkish Empire and reforming it, so that the Sultan's treatment of his

43

Christian subjects might present no pretext for Russian intervention. The Sultans proved incorrigible, but retained the wit to exploit the mutual suspicions of the powers to their own advantage. The Sick Man remained alive, his state of health a constant and irresistible topic of interest to the Tsars although their attempts to influence the making of his will brought them nothing but repeated frustration and defeat. Alexander, despite an appeal for assistance from the Serbs, had resisted the temptation during the latter half of his reign. Count Nesselrode, Nicholas's foreign minister, constantly urged upon his master the need to proceed with caution and diplomacy. He argued that the continued Turkish control of the Straits was preferable to the far worse situation which might take its place if Turkey fell and the Western powers intervened. Nicholas himself, at his coronation, assured the Duke of Wellington that he had no interest in the matter. Before long however he succumbed to its fascination and events were set in train which finally involved Russia in a ruinous war whose effects went beyond the defeat of his foreign policy to destroy much of what he had achieved at home.

His reign began with revolts by both the Roumanians and the Greeks against their Turkish overlords. For reasons of their own, both Britain and France decided to support the Greeks on this occasion and Nicholas was able to intervene without opposition. He led an army across the Danube but prudently halted his advance at Adrianople and concluded a treaty with the Sultan which affirmed self-government for the Greeks and Roumanians, annexed the mouth of the Danube and the eastern coast of the Black Sea, and promised that Russia should enjoy free passage through the Straits. A few years later the Sultan, looking for Russian protection against the ambitions of Mohammed Ali, added a further undertaking that he would close the Straits to foreign warships in time of war. The suspicious West chose to interpret this as tantamount to a Russian monopoly of the waterway and took the earliest opportunity to demand the revocation of the agreement. In 1841 Britain, France, Austria, Prussia, and Russia formed a joint protectorate over the Turkish Empire and closed the Straits to warships of all nationalities in times of peace.

These complicated agreements reflected the ascendancy of Nesselrode's cautious policy. They secured Russia's minimum aims but in the long run served only to encourage a devious but determined diplomatic contest among the powers to gain the upper hand at Constantinople. Indeed it was not Nicholas who first provoked the crisis which led to war in the 1850s but Louis Napoleon, the first Napoleon's nephew, who became the Emperor Napoleon III of France in 1852. This parvenu monarch was anxious both to consolidate his support among the Catholic population at home and to emulate his uncle's glory abroad. He found his opportunity in the unlikely setting of Palestine. Here, within the boundaries of the Turkish Empire, a handful of Orthodox monks tended the Holy Places of the Christian faith. Napoleon demanded that the keys of the Holy Places should be handed over to Catholic care. The compliant Sultan agreed but the Tsar protested and he hesitated. The British ambassador urged him not to alter his decision and the French envoy added a calculated provocation by sailing a warship through the Straits. Religion, national pride, and policy drove Nicholas to action. His armies recrossed the Danube and a Russian fleet, operating from its base at Sebastopol in the Crimea, destroyed Turkish ships in the Black Sea. The crisis rapidly escalated to war. The British government was reluctant to encourage this course but public opinion, pugnaciously expressed by *Punch*, demanded action, blaming the Tsar, of course, for what had happened.

22   The charge of the Light Brigade at Balaclava: this military blunder of spectacular bravery provided the Russian armies with their only victory in the Crimean War

23   The last act of the Crimean War: British
and French batteries bombard Sebastopol

Learn, by the case of that old brute,
    The Tsar, with pride gone mad,
That monarchy that's absolute,
    Is absolutely bad.

A combined British and French army and fleet, soon joined by the
Austrians, set sail for the mouth of the Danube. When they arrived they
discovered that the 'mad brute' had in fact prudently withdrawn his army.
The flood-tide of national prejudice was irresistible however and the allied

46

before the Russian garrison abandons this key naval
base on the shores of the Black Sea

commanders were forced to look for another target. They resolved to
destroy Sebastopol and with it Russia's whole position on the Black Sea.
They were almost totally unprepared for such a mission. Lacking reliable
maps of an area which they had not come to conquer, they inspected the
seaward defences of Sebastopol through telescopes and decided to land a
few miles to the north and attack its landward side. Their eventual landfall
found them many miles away from the fortress and separated from their
objective by a terrain of hills and valleys which it now took months to

wrest from Russian control. While they made a slow progress southwards the Russians were able to reinforce Sebastopol with both men and physical defences. After a series of battles compounded of military blunders and enormous losses on either side the allies concluded that they must settle for a long siege. They thus committed themselves to a Russian winter without winter uniforms, sufficient food and tents or medical supplies. Detailed reports by the correspondent of *The Times* soon dispelled *Punch*'s callow enthusiasm, but there was equal suffering within the Russian citadel. Communications and supplies had proved hopelessly inadequate on the Russian side too, and Russia also produced her counterpart to Florence Nightingale in the Grand Duchess Elena, the Tsar's sister-in-law, who organized a body of nurses to work under the surgeon Pirogov. Finally, in September 1855, one year after the Crimean campaign had begun, the western allies breached the defences of Sebastopol and the garrison set fire to the city and rowed away across the bay. The Crimean War was over, although peace was not signed for another year while Napoleon canvassed a scheme to march on Moscow and liberate Poland on the way. His allies prevented him from repeating his uncle's folly but thousands of men had already died to flatter his vanity. The war brought humiliating defeat to Russia, who was barred from the Danube and the Black Sea. It did nothing to solve the Eastern Question however, which nagged on to bring new confrontations in the future.

Nicholas himself died early in 1855, not living to see the fall of Sebastopol and the destruction of his own ambitions. He had already become aware of mounting discontent within his empire however and remarked to his son Alexander that 'I hand over to you my command unfortunately not in as good order as I would have wished'. The war had been the principal agent in precipitating the turbulent state in which his reign closed. The western invasion had closed the export route for grain and thus set off an adverse economic reaction which was partially responsible for many of the 400 peasant risings which had occurred in recent years. In doing so it also drew attention to the fact that the basic problems of serfdom remained unchanging after half a century. The population of Russia was rising rapidly, but both the agricultural and the social systems lagged behind. For all his devotion to Russian tradition, Nicholas had realized the evils of serfdom. He showed his concern by setting up a ministry to deal with state peasants which encouraged improved farming methods, built hospitals, and opened primary schools. The progress made had been little enough however; the number of hospitals built by 1865 was twice what it had been ten years earlier, but was still only twenty-five, and just over 100,000 children were enrolled in the schools. Private serfdom moreover had remained untouched. Nicholas hoped to see its end in time but argued that he could do nothing until the climate of opinion among the landowners had changed. He ended the splitting up of families and sale in the market-place but continued the practice of transferring large numbers of state peasants to private ownership. By 1855, as we have seen, even the proverbial patience of the Russian peasant was nearing exhaustion and braver spirits were beginning to take their salvation into their own hands, although Nicholas's government responded with time-honoured harshness by flogging the leaders and conscripting them into the ranks of the armed forces who went to fight and die in the Crimea.

The war also served to reveal the inefficiency and the corruption of the administration, something which had long been evident to anyone privileged to read the reports of the Third Department. Some of the bureaucrats themselves were coming to realize the need for change, although their schemes stood little chance of success without the personal blessing of the Tsar. Nicholas would delegate nothing except to secret committees, for which he had a passion amounting to mania. All state papers had to pass through His Majesty's Own Chancery, where they mounted in piles around the bust of Peter the Great while administrative congestion added to the general inefficiency of government. Above all the war revealed for everyone to see the gap which existed between Russia and the West. For all their mistakes, the Western powers had proved too strong for Russia. Until she could match their war-machine, her foreign ambitions remained vain hopes. The first steps in such a much-needed transformation must be made at the heart of the social and political system.

This was the opinion not only of highly-placed officials but also of the majority of educated men. That majority remained a tiny minority in Russia as a whole, of course, but the grim efforts of the Third Department had not been able to erase the marks of Western thought upon the Russian mind, although they had succeeded in silencing many thinkers and driving others into exile. An intelligentsia was beginning to grow in Russia in the first half of the nineteenth century and social and political discussions continued if only at an underground and theoretical level. The policy of indoctrination pursued by the régime met with some success however in determining the direction of some of this discussion. The intelligentsia

49

24 A convoy of prisoners, bound for Siberia, halts
exhausted on the barren road which Russians said
was 'worn out by chains'

was divided into two schools of thought, equally discontented with the
present but disagreeing about the correct course of action for the future.
The Slavophils, as they were called, remained true to their Orthodox and
nationalist education by regarding Russia as irrevocably separate from
Europe. They argued that Russia could learn nothing from the West but
must seek salvation along the path determined by her culture and her history. In particular they placed their hopes upon the peasants and the village
commune, a traditional gathering of elders which for ages had met to deter-
mine the pace of the agricultural year upon the open fields, periodically
redistributing the scattered holdings to ensure rough justice. The com-

mune, the Slavophils argued, could become the basis of democracy in Russia, avoiding the pitfalls of competitive individualism and *laisser-faire* industrialism into which western Europe had fallen. It was a pious hope, but the Slavophils were devoutly religious men.

The second school of thought, known since as the Westernizers, poured scorn upon this romanticism. In their view the Russian past contained everything which was responsible for her present backwardness. Autocracy and serfdom were the basic evils, but the commune was a contributory factor, introduced by the Tsars to keep the peasants in their place. Among the most eloquent of the Westernizers were men such as Peter Chadayev, Vissarion Belinsky, and Alexander Herzen. Chadayev was the most scornful critic of Russian traditionalism while Belinsky, the son of a country priest, declared roundly that the Orthodox Church 'has always been the bulwark of the whip and the handmaid of despotism'. It was for disseminating Belinsky's views that Dostoevsky was arrested by the Third Department. Alexander Herzen was the illegitimate son of a landowner, whose outspoken views forced him to go into exile early in his life. From the security of western Europe he launched an indictment of Nicholas himself:

> Nicholas I follows the traditions of Peter the Great in his foreign policy but suppresses them at home. Which means that, while the territory and importance of the Empire increase, its public life is reduced to less than nothing. Everything is done for the throne, nothing for the people. The Emperor is no more than a military man, and all the attempts at education and culture initiated by Peter are simply thwarted. The Western ideas of human dignity, freedom and justice must be applied to Russian life; serfdom must be abolished, the whole régime transformed into a constitutional, liberal and democratic monarchy or republic. All the talk about Russian humility and orthodoxy is merely helping the reaction; the future of the country lies not in the resurrection of Byzantine prejudices or pseudo-national smugness, but in free thought, science, individual and collective liberty and the transformation of the social and economic order.

This argument about Russia's national character went deep into her past and was to continue in the future. Whether Russia should have anything to do with Europe or retain her isolation was to be a root cause of the bitter quarrel between the Communists Stalin and Trotsky in the twentieth century. At the end of Nicholas's reign the question presented Russia with a crisis. The situation was more truly revolutionary than that of the Decembrist conspiracy in which he had ascended the throne. It was left to his son Alexander to find an answer.

25   Alexander II, the Tsar who liberated the serfs
and was himself assassinated by a Nihilist bomb

4 The Tsar Liberator

It is better to abolish serfdom from above than to wait until the serfs begin to liberate themselves from below.

THESE WORDS, spoken by the Tsar Alexander II (1855–81) to an assembly of the Moscow nobility soon after his accession, supply the vital clue to the thinking of the man who now took the step before which his predecessors had hesitated for a century. With a rare flash of imagination, Nicholas had deliberately set out to ensure that his son's apprenticeship to tsardom should be more thorough than his own. For ten years or more Alexander had sat in committees and read the reports of the Third Department and he was in no doubt, when he came to the throne, of the rising tension throughout the empire. Indeed, he brought the Crimean War to an end in order to be free to deal with the problem. A true Romanov, he abandoned none of Russia's ambitions in the Black Sea or the Balkans but realized also the changes which had become necessary before Russia could challenge the West upon equal terms. No doubt humanitarian motives also played their part. His aunt Elena and his brother Constantine were both convinced reformers whose influence upon the new Tsar was considerable. In the last analysis however it was the threat of social revolution which weighed heaviest in his decision. Alexander acted because of the dangers of inactivity. He took a risk, but it was less than the risk involved in doing nothing.

One danger no longer existed however. The opposition of the landowners to emancipation, which had defeated Catherine, discouraged Alexander I, and persuaded Nicholas to postpone a decision, was now rapidly diminishing. For the nobles, as for the Tsar, the facts of life were no doubt the most potent argument. The rising wave of murders of landowners and their bailiffs continued unabated in the early years of the new reign and self-preservation dictated a change in their relationship with the peasants. The growth of humanitarian feeling had also influenced them. A generation of Russian novelists like Gogol and Ivan Turgenev had attacked the demoralizing influence of serfdom upon masters and servants alike. No Russian novel had appeared to compare with Harriet Beecher Stowe's bitter attack upon American slavery in *Uncle Tom's Cabin*, and in any case the censorship would never have allowed its publication. The Russian novelists had used the weapon of satire, however, subtler and perhaps more effective in its impact. For, while *Uncle Tom's Cabin* served only to enrage the American slave-owners and deepen their determination to retain their 'peculiar institution', the readers of Gogol and Turgenev became ashamed of their image as stupid and unconsciously sadistic tyrants. In his novel *Dead Souls* Gogol painted a picture of the Russian gentry class as ignorant and miserly men and women who fell easy prey to a quick-witted scoundrel named Chichikov. Chichikov travelled about among them obtaining, either through glib persuasion or in return for small sums of money, lists of the names of those of their peasants who had recently died. Equipped with this list of non-existent serfs, he planned to raise a mortgage on his 'property'. The serfs themselves, whether living or dead, hardly feature in his story as real persons. They have no existence except as the dumb possessions of their masters and mistresses. Gogol escaped the censor because of his wit. Even Nicholas I himself laughed aloud when the manuscript was read to him. The poet Pushkin, on the other hand, sighed 'God, how sad our Russia is'. Turgenev, who painted similar but more sombre pictures of serfdom in his novels and short stories, was less fortunate in his personal career. He was accused of 'ridiculing the landowners, presenting them in a light derogatory to their honour, and in general propagating opinions detrimental to the respect due to the nobility from the other classes'. He was imprisoned and subsequently confined to his estates for a year. His personal fate indicates the impact which his books had made, however, and Alexander II later told him that his novels had been one of the factors which led to his own decision to emancipate the serfs.

For less sensitive landowners the old economic arguments no longer applied. Russia was no longer short of labour and many areas, including the steppes, were becoming overpopulated. Landowners there, concerned only with maximizing the profitability of their estates through the export trade in grain, had come to realize that serfdom was economically inefficient. Serfs and their families occupied valuable land and slowed up production by their archaic methods and their part-time, unenthusiastic labour. A wage-labour force would be both cheaper and more efficient. Landowners in the less fertile and, in some places, exhausted farmlands of

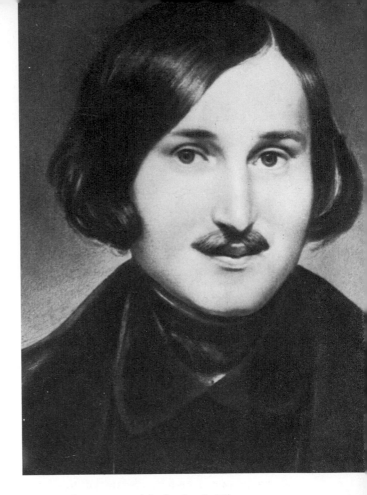

26 Nicholas Gogol, the 'Russian Dickens', whose novel *Dead Souls* did much to discredit serfdom and the rural society which it supported

the centre and the west were more ready to part with the land. They were less eager to lose their serfs however, chiefly because they themselves were deep in debt and had mortgaged their human property like the fictitious Chichikov. Several years had therefore to be spent in haggling and discussion between the Tsar and the nobles before a satisfactory bargain could be struck. In 1861 however, two years before the emancipation of the American slaves, Alexander declared the end of serfdom in Russia.

The land problem had been solved by a compromise. Serfs were to be set free without compensation to the landlords for the loss of their labour. They were to receive the plots of land immediately surrounding their houses. How much more they retained of the land which they had formerly tilled depended upon the landlord's readiness to part with it and the decisions of local arbitrators, chosen as a rule from among the landowning

27 Emancipation was only the beginning of
Russia's agricultural revolution. Late in the nineteenth century, a peasant continues to till the soil
with his wooden, horse-drawn plough

class. For the loss of this land the landowner would be generously compensated. The rates were generally fixed far above the current market value of
the land. Four-fifths of this sum would be advanced immediately by the
state in cash or bonds. The remaining one-fifth must be paid by the peasant,
who would repay the outstanding sum to the state over a period of forty-
nine years. The Tsar was satisfied with this scheme, because both landowners and serfs received something from it. To have liberated the serfs
without land would have made the probability of revolution even more
imminent. From the government's point of view a second problem still
remained however. The head of the Third Department had once described the serf-owner as 'the natural police magistrate, the unsleeping
watchdog of the state'. Who would now be responsible for controlling the
rural population, conscripting soldiers, collecting the poll-tax and the new redemption payments? For these tasks the Tsar called on the commune, which
was given much greater legal powers. The elders of the commune became
responsible for all the tasks which the landlord had previously performed
for the state. Slavophil thinking had achieved at least one practical success.

56

All these provisions were announced in an imperial edict which ended with some cautionary words:

And now we confidently hope that the freed serfs, in the presence of the new future which is opened before them, will appreciate and recognize the considerable sacrifices which the nobility has made on their behalf. . . .

Only by assiduous labour, a rational expenditure of their strength and resources, a strict economy, and, above all, by an upright life – a life constantly inspired by the fear of the Lord – can they hope for prosperity and progress.

And now, my orthodox and faithful people, make the holy sign of the cross and join thy prayers to ours, invoking the blessing of the Most High upon the first of thy free labours, for this alone is a sure pledge of private well-being and the public weal.

The old note of divinely inspired paternalism thus echoes through the most radical reform which a Tsar had introduced. There is also, perhaps, a note of apprehension. The Tsar's words seem less confident than he claimed. He had gambled on the future. What would be the peasants' response?

In fact it contained the time-honoured elements of apathy, suspicion, and resentment. Some peasants disliked change for its own sake. It must be remembered that many serfs had enjoyed a quiet and idle subsistence under their former masters. 'The Russian peasant', a proverb ran, 'could get the better of God Himself.' Many had got the better of their masters and did not relish the personal responsibilities of freedom. Those who did, on the other hand, soon found fresh reasons for discontent under the new system. Many were left with less land than before. No amount of legal explanation, let alone the Tsar's pious exhortations, could convince them that they had not been robbed of what was rightfully theirs. The land-scheme, moreover, had contained a clause allowing a landowner, if he wished, to make a minimum grant of land without payment or compensation. This arrangement had proved particularly popular in the fertile steppes. Even the law referred to these grants as 'beggarly allotments' and many of the new owners faced poverty from the start. Household serfs had been given no land at all and from now on constituted a rural proletariat, dependent upon wage-labour and increasingly ready to revolt against their condition as the years passed. Many of the peasants who had gained substantial acreage could raise the money to pay for it only by returning to work for the old master. Others rented extra land from him and paid for it with half their crops. Finally the most enterprising of the new peasant-farmers discovered that they had exchanged the old master for a new one

28 A country fair during Holy Week. Festivals like this one were the great occasions in the dreary monotony of peasant and provincial life

far more interfering and oppressive. If they wished to consolidate their land, the commune frequently demanded a return to the old system of scattered holdings and periodic redistribution. If they farmed profitably, then the commune raised their tax-assessment accordingly. Without a passport from the commune it was illegal for them to leave the neighbourhood. To Slavophil intellectuals the commune represented all that was best and most promising in Russian life but to many farmers it brought only frustration. Democracy in this form left them at the mercy of their least progressive and most jealous neighbours.

In many ways therefore emancipation failed to live up to the peasants'

expectations and in some it left them worse off than before. Nevertheless it represented a personal triumph for Alexander II. Indeed, in some respects his achievement was greater than that of Abraham Lincoln or his successors. America freed the slaves only as the result of a civil war but Alexander forestalled a revolution by emancipating the serfs. Unlike the American reformers, who consigned the Blacks to penury and left their former owners sullen and resentful, he laid the foundations for a new life for the peasants and won the consent of the landowners to his doing so. He also set in motion an economic revolution. The export trade in grain leapt forward. Wage-labour in the countryside introduced a money economy and a domestic market for Russian industry, which now began a revolution of its own. Millions of peasants, despite the passport restrictions, began to move into the towns to form an industrial labour-force. In all these ways Alexander's reform did more than give legal freedom to the

59

peasants. It liberated Russia as a whole from the shackles of feudalism and subsistence farming and began the development of a modern economy and society.

With serfdom gone, would the absolute power of tsardom follow? More than one assembly of nobles, summoned to discuss the business of emancipation, had proceeded to debate the case for a Russian parliament. The leaders in these discussions had been imprisoned in the Peter-Paul fortress, however. Alexander had no intention of becoming a constitutional monarch. He had abolished serfdom in order to preserve tsardom, not to destroy it. He made some further reforms in the system of local government in the years following emancipation, but these must be regarded as the inevitable administrative consequences of his great reform rather than as steps towards democracy. District and provincial councils were created, known as *zemstvos*, composed of elected representatives of the nobility and the communes. A similar system of representative govern-

29   The emancipation of the serfs: the liberal landowner Tolstoy is called in to redistribute the land between the unyielding proprietor and the bewildered and disgruntled peasants who were formerly his serfs

ment was established in the principal cities a few years later. These assemblies were forbidden to discuss political questions, however, and had no powers in relation to the central government. Subjects such as farming techniques, veterinary services, hospitals, and primary schools occupied their attention. The zemstvos were in fact created to take over responsibilities which had once been the vague obligations of landlords but which were too big for the communes and too widespread to be left to the central government. A similar motive lay behind the new institution of Justices of the Peace. These officials, elected by the zemstvos, took over the petty courts which landowners had previously held. In their consequences, however, and even to some extent, perhaps, in their intentions, these reforms marked something more than a mere re-organization of Russian government. The reform of the judicial system, for instance, was accompanied by the introduction of the jury system in criminal cases, an important change for which Russia had been waiting since the century began. Like the establishment of the elective principle in local government, this was an important step forward in Russian social development. Like emancipation itself, these changes took time to make their full effects apparent. Neither the zemstvos nor the new judicial system operated freely, both because of constant interference from the central government and opposition from powerful individuals who countermanded their decisions and bribed judges. In the long run however the reforms of Alexander's reign were to achieve more than he himself intended. Emancipation, as has been explained, marked the beginning of an economic and social revolution. The zemstvos, for all their limitations, gave Russia an apprenticeship in self-government. Nobles naturally took the leading places in them, particularly in the provincial assemblies. Equally naturally, these men tended to be the most energetic and progressive members of their class, since no others would accept the responsibilities involved. The zemstvos thus produced a new type of Russian nobleman, a man with an independent mind and political and administrative experience. Within fifty years these men demanded a Russian parliament and, when the last Tsar was forced by circumstances to grant their request, they occupied the leading places in the parliament as an organized party with a coherent and radical programme of political and social reform. Thus Alexander had unintentionally laid the foundations of constitutional government in Russia. Not only had serfdom gone, but tsardom also could never be quite the same again.

Within his own lifetime and as the consequence of his actions Alexander

61

30 Moscow in the nineteenth century: a mixture
of modern buildings and the frowning medieval
walls of the Kremlin

met the fate which can so often befall men who challenge the dead hand of
tradition and release the forces of change. He asked for co-operation, if not
for gratitude, but received instead impatient criticism. Reactionaries reproached him for stirring up trouble. As though to prove their pessimism
justified, both peasants and reforming nobles grumbled that he had not
done enough for them. His sternest and least tolerant critics came from the
student population however. In 1861, just after emancipation, university
students in St Petersburg, Moscow, and Kazan demonstrated against everything from the examination system and lack of participation in university
government to the conditions of the serfs. These students were members of
a new wave in Russia. Less disciplined and repressed than their parents
under Nicholas I, they were more outspoken in their criticism of the régime
and more extreme in their ideas for the future. Even their appearance was
designed to draw attention to them and to mark them out as rebels against

tradition. They wore long hair and beards, both frowned upon in the previous reign, slouch hats, and long scarves draped negligently around their necks and shoulders. To the older generation they appeared rootless and shiftless, despising everything and believing in nothing. The novelist Turgenev coined a name for them which was to stick: Nihilists.

> "He is a Nihilist," Arcady repeated.
> "A Nihilist," his father said slowly. "As far as I can judge, that must be a word derived from the Latin *nihil – nothing*; the term must therefore signify a man who . . . will admit nothing?"
> " Better still – a man who will respect nothing," Paul Petrovich interjected, and then resumed his buttering.
> "Who looks at everything critically," Arcady remarked.
> "And what is the difference?" his uncle inquired.
> "There is a difference. A Nihilist is a man who admits no established authorities, who takes no principles for granted, however much they may be respected."
> "Well then? Is that a good thing?" his uncle interrupted.
> "That depends on the circumstances, uncle. It's good in some cases and very bad in others."[1]

Few Nihilists made Arcady's reservations in real life however. They condemned not only serfdom but also Alexander's reforms. Nothing less than the abolition of tsardom would satisfy them. They were also opposed to the influence of religion in Russia. These opinions make them seem very similar to the Westernizers of the previous reign. The Nihilists however were far more extreme than the reformers of the older generation both in their plans for the future and their methods of seeking to achieve their ends. They were very much influenced by the ideas of Karl Marx which were beginning to infiltrate the European underground. Marx was chiefly concerned with the industrial society of western Europe. He argued that the factory workers there, exploited and impoverished by their capitalist employers, could and inevitably would unite to overthrow their oppressors by violent revolution. A new society, classless and co-operative, would rise from the ruins of class-ridden and competitive capitalism. The Russian radicals realized that the classes of which he spoke hardly existed as yet in Russia, but developed from the basis of his ideas, and under the equal influence of Slavophilism, a revolutionary theory of their own. The peasants were the heroes of this ideology and the landowners the villains. The village commune took the place of the factory as the revolutionary cell. The new Russian society which they envisaged would be based upon the

[1] Turgenev: *Fathers and Sons.*

common ownership of the land. Indeed, they dreamed that Russia might perhaps avoid altogether the evils of industrialization and proceed to the Marxist ideal of anarchist communism by a superior path of her own. In their own phrase, they wanted Russia to 'say her own word'.

In the summer of 1873 and 1874 hundreds of young men and women left their universities and went into the countryside to preach their revolutionary ideas. The peasants paused in their labours, laid down their rustic implements and listened. A few were interested but most were too ignorant to understand what the excited students were talking about. Their combination of educated accents and scruffy appearance seemed odd and sinister. A peasant could recognize a gentleman or a gypsy, but not a young man who talked like one and looked like the other. They were particularly shocked by the free talk and behaviour of the girls. No peasant woman would dare to talk and act like this. The peasants reported the student 'Populists' to the police and they were arrested. The speeches of their defending counsel made far more effective propaganda for their ideas but most of them were deported to Siberia. The survivors paused and thought again. It had become clear that they could not rely upon the spontaneous action of the peasants. Organization was needed. A society was formed, called 'Land and Liberty', and its members went to the people again in 1877 with more success. They adopted Pugachov's old tactics, shrewdly proclaiming that it was the Tsar's wish that his people should rise against the landlords. They enlisted about 1,000 peasants and drilled them for rebellion. A drunken peasant leaked the plan however and arrests and disorder followed. Organization paid one bonus. Some members of the society who had escaped arrest were able to launch a successful raid to liberate the leaders from their prison in Kiev.

It was one of Russia's ironies that her revolutionaries could only succeed in winning support at this stage of history by invoking the authority of the Tsar. Tsardom still dominated Russian life and her imagination. For this reason a second type of Nihilist became obsessed with the idea that Russia could never be liberated while the Tsar lived. If the whole of the Russian system of society and government depended upon the will of one man, they argued, then only by removing him could the system be radically changed. From this argument developed a series of attempts upon the life of the Tsar which came to an end only when it succeeded. 'Am I a wild beast that they should hound me to death?' protested the outraged and embittered monarch.

64

The anarchist assassins were passionate and wild idealists such as perhaps only Russia could have produced at this stage in history. Serge Nechayev was a school-teacher, the son of a workman, who believed that in order to build it was first necessary to destroy. In practice he achieved nothing except the murder of an accomplice suspected of being a police-agent. At his trial and during a long imprisonment in the Peter-Paul fortress from 1872–82 he showed great courage and became a hero to Nihilists perhaps chiefly because he had maintained the purity of his motives by his failure in action. Vera Zasulich was a young woman who in 1878, after the trial and sentence of fellow-Nihilists, walked into the office of St Petersburg's chief of police and shot him. He recovered and she was put on trial but acquitted by a jury. As she left the court she was smuggled away through the crowd before the police could re-arrest her. Stephen Khalturin, the son of a peasant and founder of the Northern Union of Russian Workers, obtained work as a labourer in the Winter Palace. He slept with dynamite under his pillow and, when the opportunity presented itself, planted the explosive in the state dining-room a few hours before the

31   The first attempt on the life of Alexander II: firemen arrive to deal with the explosion in the state dining-room at the Winter Palace

Tsar was due to entertain the Prince of Bulgaria. The Prince was late and the dinner was delayed. The explosion occurred however and killed or wounded scores of footmen and guards. Sophie Perovskaya illustrates the generation gap in a particularly vivid way, for she was the daughter of a former governor of St Petersburg. A frail and beautiful girl, she was responsible for planning two attempts on the life of Alexander II. In 1880 mines were laid to derail and destroy the Imperial train but failed to explode. In 1881 a last plan succeeded and Sophie Perovskaya was among those executed for their part in it.

Faced as it was with this wave of terrorism and, in 1863, by a new Polish revolt, it is hardly surprising that Alexander's government became increasingly repressive as the years went by. Police powers were increased and, after the Zasulich affair, all cases of 'resistance to the authorities, rebellion, assassination or attempts on the lives of officials' were revoked from trial by jury to be heard by military courts. To Alexander's credit however, although he had far more personal cause for tyranny than his predecessors, he continued to give thought to the possibilities of reform. Early in 1881 his advisers laid before him a plan to associate elected representatives of the zemstvos with the central Council of State. This was not a scheme to bring constitutional government to Russia, since the function of the new councillors would be purely advisory. Like Alexander's other reforms however this scheme would inevitably have tended to give the Russian people a greater interest and a greater share in the government of their country. Alexander prepared to sign the document in the first week of March. On 1 March he drove through the streets, apparently in good spirits, on his way back to the Winter Palace after attending a military parade. A bomb was thrown and shattered his carriage. The Tsar stepped out to enquire about injuries to his escort and to see the young Nihilist who had been arrested. Another bomb arched across the snow and he fell back, this time mortally wounded. He died in the palace a few hours later and with him, it may be said, died most of Russia's hopes for a peaceful future. Alexander's limited reforms had opened up a gap between Russia's social and political development. His successors made no attempt to bridge it for the rest of the nineteenth century, but rather tried to recover the ground which had already been surrendered. Succeeding generations of would-be reformers, therefore, their hopes of constitutional government apparently irrevocably dashed, turned increasingly to the study of the theory and practice of revolutionary violence.

32 The Nihilists succeed, and Alexander is
borne away to die in the Winter Palace. The
scheme for constitutional reform which awaited
his signature will now never be signed

5 Reaction and Change

THE SEQUEL to Alexander II's assassination immediately revealed the fallacy in the Nihilists' argument. Although the revolutionaries gave their tiny organizations grand-sounding names such as 'The People's Reckoning' and 'The People's Will', the Russian people did not respond to them and their actions succeeded only in provoking a furious backlash of opinion among those in power. Alexander III, the second son of Alexander II, who now succeeded to the throne (1881–94) was a strong and unimaginative man who had never approved of the reforms of his father's reign and now became even more certain that it was his duty to repair the damage which had been done to tsardom. The first proclamation of his reign declared that

> The voice of God orders us to stand boldly by the task of governing, relying on Divine Providence, with faith in the strength and truth of autocratic power, which we have been called to confirm and protect for the good of the people, against all encroachments.

To be accurate, these were the words of the Tsar's former tutor, Count Constantine Pobedonostsev, Procurator of the Holy Synod and an orthodox Russian in every sense of the word. His influence predominated at court. The proclamation was published without the remaining ministers of Alexander II having been consulted or even informed. They were soon dismissed from office and their paper schemes went with them. In the next fifteen years the new government did its best to undo the effects of most of the reforms which had been accomplished. The Justices of the Peace were replaced by Land Commandants, officials appointed by the Minister of the Interior with combined judicial and administrative powers, able to overrule both the zemstvos and the communes. The zemstvos remained in existence because they had already taken root too deeply to be altogether destroyed. Their membership was now restricted to members of the nobility however and they were subjected to increasing interference and control. In cities and towns the property and occupational qualification for voting was raised. The total electorate in St Petersburg dropped by two-thirds as a

33 The years of reaction begin, as the leading
Nihilists are executed after the assassination of
Alexander II

result. Universities were subjected directly to government control and un-
desirable students were expelled. The old policy of religious indoctrination
was reintroduced and extended throughout the empire. In recent years the
slackening of the Tsar's grip at the centre had encouraged the growth of
nationalist feelings at the fringes, resulting, for instance, in a new Polish
revolt in 1863. Polish government was now directly subjected to Russia
and a determined attempt was made not merely to suppress Polish nationalism but to kill it. Russian became the official language for everything except
religious instruction and Catholic monasteries were closed. The Orthodox
Church began intensive missionary activity. The same happened in the
Baltic States, the Ukraine, and the Asiatic territories of the empire. The
limited rights of self-government which Finland had enjoyed were whittled
down and the country progressively incorporated within the Russian state.
One religious minority within the empire suffered a particularly unpleasant

34   Reaction continues, as a peasant tries to present
a petition to the Tsar but is pulled away by
Cossacks and police

experience. In 1881 the first *pogrom* took place in Russia: a violent mass-destruction of Jewish property in the cities of Odessa and Kiev, accompanied by physical attacks on Jewish people. Neither Alexander nor Pobedonostsev liked the Jews and when the government finally intervened it was only to limit their liberties still more stringently. They were barred from living outside large towns and restricted to practising certain trades. The number of university places open to them was limited and their right to vote in zemstvo elections was withdrawn.

In this one respect, the development of anti-semitic prejudice, Russia might be said to have been ahead of the rest of Europe at the end of the nineteenth century. This was the period of the Dreyfus affair in France and when Adolf Hitler was barely in his teens, living in the cosmopolitan city of Vienna, but only in Russia were Jews beginning to experience the active persecution which was to be their fate all over the continent in the first half of the twentieth century. It was in Russia that the rumour began to spread that the Elders of Zion were engaged in a conspiracy to subvert and take over Europe. In almost every other respect however Russia's backwardness seemed to be confirmed and almost encouraged by the government. Agriculture continued to develop at a snail's pace, still hampered by peasant ignorance and the restrictions of the commune. At the beginning of spring the village priest appeared to sprinkle the furrows and the cattle with holy water and from then on peasant families laboured in the fields from dawn until dusk to raise the harvest upon which the payment of their rent, redemption dues, and taxes depended. Education, at the primary level, stagnated. In spite of the efforts of the zemstvos, at the end of the century four Russians in five were still unable either to read or write.

In many ways, therefore, Russia under Alexander III seemed almost to be moving backward into the period of Nicholas I. There was more than a similarity between the fate of Fedor Dostoevsky and that of Alexander Ulyanov, the elder son of a gentleman of the Simbirsk province, who was arrested for implication in a plot against the Tsar and hanged, in 1887, at the age of nineteen. The sequel however was significant. Alexander's younger brother, Vladimir, seems even at the age of seventeen to have been converted into a revolutionary. Thus a career began which was to end with the destruction of tsarist autocracy and the establishment of a Communist state in Russia. This incident symbolizes what was really happening in Russia during Alexander's reign. The country was in movement beneath

35   A blast furnace in the Urals signals the beginning
of Russia's industrial revolution

36 The Russian proletariat comes to life in the
1890s: the first generation of industrial workers,
men, women, and children, gather in the factories
of Moscow

the still surface which the Tsar and his tutor sought to impose and it was
not possible to turn the clock back half a century. Indeed, this was obvious
to any traveller in the country. Railways were beginning to cross the vast
countryside and shorten its distances. In many towns and cities, the chim-
neys of factories and mills were beginning to rise above the gilded domes of
churches and monasteries. Russia's industrial revolution, which had been
made possible by the reform of Alexander II's reign, had been set in
motion. Ironically, the men most responsible for these changes were
members of the Tsar's own government.

Nicholas Bunge, Minister of Finance from 1878–86, I.A. Vyshnegradsky, who followed him, and Sergius Witte, whose term of office began in Alexander's reign but continued and reached its climax in that of his successor, Nicholas II, were none of them typical figures of tsarist government, which perhaps accounts to some extent for their forward-looking views. Bunge was a former professor of economics and Vyshnegradsky, although the son of a priest, was a businessman. Witte was the son of a German or Dutch Protestant and himself married a Jewish divorcee. It was under the guidance and inspiration of these three men that the industrial transformation of Russia began and right from the start, therefore, the process was different from that which western Europe had experienced. The state, not private enterprise, took the initiative. A State Bank provided capital and major industries developed as state monopolies. The state purchased existing railways and constructed new ones. The state created steamship companies, polytechnics, and engineering institutes. It is possible to wonder whether, in backward Russia, an industrial revolution would have begun at all without this governmental impetus and some scholars minimize the importance of what was achieved under what they regard as artificial conditions. Statistics suggest that it was crucial however. Between 1880 and 1914 coal output multiplied more than ten times, iron ore production by roughly the same amount, and a steel industry came into existence. The production of petroleum for sale in foreign markets and use in the industrial region of Moscow tripled in the last decade of the nineteenth century and textiles doubled in the same period. It is true that these figures represent a start from virtually nothing and that the textile industry, by the time of the First World War, was still less mechanized than that of Lancashire. Nevertheless the start had been made. It is equally arguable that what set Russia back was the period of revolution and civil war which followed and from which the country was rescued, under Communism, only by an even more intensive system of state control.

What remain beyond dispute are the social and, ultimately, the political consequences of these changes in the late nineteenth century. Railway and telegraphic communications broke down the rural isolation of old Russia and carried both men and ideas, as well as raw materials and industrial products, throughout the empire. In Russia, moreover, as everywhere else in Europe during a period of industrial revolution, the people paid the price of change and counted the cost. The first victims were the peasants. Already burdened with rent and redemption payments, they were now obliged to meet the cost of the government's policy through high tariffs on foreign imports and taxes on consumer goods such as kerosene, sugar, matches, and vodka which they used every day. Their restlessness increased and the Populists found more willing audiences for their revolutionary ideas. Those peasants who left the countryside and travelled along the rivers and the railways to find employment in the industrial centres found, on their arrival, the apparently inevitable conditions of early industrialization which the West was beginning to leave behind. Long hours at dangerous machines for low wages became the common experience of men, women, and children and housing was squalid and over-crowded. Both Bunge and Witte enacted laws to limit hours of work, particularly for children, but like similar codes in the West these were opposed and evaded by employers. A tsarist government required little encouragement to de-

37 Plekhanov, the father of
Russian Marxism

clare trade unions illegal and Cossacks found a new duty in clearing the
streets of working-class demonstrators.

Industrial society in Russia developed a special feature however which
made it different from that of the West. Because of the artificial and state-
controlled manner in which industry arose, it was concentrated chiefly into
a few cities, such as St Petersburg and Moscow in the west and Odessa
in the south, and into a relatively small number of big factories. Combined with the savage social conditions, therefore, the development of
industry in Russia produced a situation unique in Europe at the end of the
nineteenth century. Russia, which Marx had dismissed from his calculations
as an irrevocably feudal and rural society, in fact evolved the conditions
which he described as the basis for proletarian revolution. Class differences
in Russia were bleak and uncompromising. The condition of the workers
was desperate and police repression was savage. At the same time, the
armies of revolution had been created in the huge factories. Russia, more
than any country except perhaps Italy or Spain at the same period,

38   The founders of the St Petersburg Union for
the Liberation of the Working Class. The high
forehead and unyielding glance of the young Lenin
already dominate the revolutionary scene

presented the Marxist with his opportunity. Among the first to realize this
was George Plekhanov, the son of a nobleman and a member of the first
Nihilist generation. In his student days Plekhanov was a Populist but soon
realized both the uselessness of terrorist tactics and the significance of the

industrial revolution. The greater part of his life was spent in exile, a circumstance which perhaps gave added perspective to his views of the Russian scene. In 1883, with Vera Zasulich and others, he founded in Geneva a party called the 'Liberation of Labour' which was uncompromisingly Marxist in its programme. By the end of the century it was becoming active in Russia itself and the younger Ulyanov, now better known under his revolutionary pseudonym of Lenin, was one of Plekhanov's keenest disciples, although he was to prove even more impatient than his master in his insistence upon the need for proletarian revolution. While Plekhanov, the orthodox Marxist, felt that capitalism in Russia must be allowed to run its course and produce a Russian parliament before the proletarians had their turn, Lenin argued that Russian conditions made it unnecessary to wait.

One day in 1888 the Tsar and his heir-apparent, his son Nicholas, came near to becoming victims of industrialization in a different way. The Imperial train was derailed, not by the work of terrorists but by chance. More than twenty people were killed in the crash but Alexander himself, a huge man possessed of great physical strength, supported the sagging timbers of the royal carriage while Nicholas crawled to safety. It is tempting to see in this incident a metaphor for the reign: the Tsar supporting by his personal effort the tottering fabric of his régime. This would however be an exaggeration. When Alexander died peacefully in 1894 he had good reason to be content that he had succeeded in the task which he, or rather, in his estimation, the Almighty, had set himself. Although the peasants were known to be suffering and the Tsar himself reproached his finance ministers for contributing to their misery, the political scene was outwardly quiet. The zemstvos were quiescent and the Cossacks controlled the streets. The churches and the prisons were full. In foreign affairs also, as will shortly be explained, his reign had ended with success for Russia. Nevertheless it remains true that deep-rooted and far-reaching changes were taking place in Russia, changes which the Tsar himself did not understand. These changes, however, were eroding the whole basis of tsardom and creating a situation which the old methods of autocracy would be hard put to control in the years which were to come. Nicholas I had instinctively distrusted railways. Both literally and figuratively they replaced the old, static, Russia by a society on the move. Self-confident men of business were more difficult to browbeat and deny than bucolic squires. A seething mass of industrial workers presented problems for the police far more difficult

77

than those involved in controlling traditionally subservient peasants tightly organized in isolated village communities. The old religious orthodoxies exercised an appeal upon fewer and fewer minds in competition with the scientific arguments of Marxism. Although Pobedonostsev lived on to influence the attitudes and the policies of the new reign, his traditional answers were to prove less and less applicable to new and unprecedented questions.

The changes which had taken place in foreign policy constituted no less a revolution than that which was taking place within Russia. Indeed, a dramatic transformation had taken place in the European balance of power since the end of the Crimean War. The leading agent of this revolution was Otto von Bismarck, the chief minister of Prussia. Between 1860 and 1870, while Alexander II wrestled with the problems of emancipation, Bismarck defeated first Austria and then Napoleon III of France in swift and devastating military campaigns and created a German Empire, with Prussia at its head. After this Bismarck ceased to be a revolutionary in any sense and concentrated upon suppressing the forces of liberalism, Catholicism, and socialism within his new empire, while repairing his external relations with Austria and isolating France from the other powers of Europe so that she could not contemplate a war of revenge. To this end he wished to bring Russia back into the concert of powers and formed, in 1873, the 'League of the Three Emperors' of Russia, Germany, and Austria, a pale imitation of the Holy Alliance which had been destroyed by the Crimean War and with none of that organization's pious aspirations. The first reaction of Alexander II to the Franco–Prussian War of 1870 however was to recover some of what Napoleon III had taken away, while Napoleon and Europe were engaged elsewhere. In 1870 he announced his abrogation of the Paris treaty of 1856 and put Russian warships back on the Black Sea. For the moment the West could do nothing but agree.

Alexander II's foreign Minister, Prince Gorchakov, was a man in the mould of Nesselrode, anxious to avoid ruinous confrontations with the West. A new mood of nationalism was sweeping the country however, inspired by Nicholas's deliberate encouragement of nationalism and the Slavophils. 'Pan-Slavism', as it is known, was a programme to unite all the Balkan peoples under the general leadership of Russia. Before long it committed the Tsars to new adventures in the Balkans which Gorchakov could only try to control as best he might. In 1875 the Sultan's tax-gatherers appeared in Bosnia and Herzegovina, two provinces to the west of the now independent Serbia, and the people rose in revolt. Serbia soon declared war on Turkey and the Bulgars joined in the rising. The Sultan called in Circassian cavalry to suppress the rising with terrible atrocities and Russian volunteers made the sign of the Cross and left for the Balkans. The Tsar could not stay out for long and in 1877 a Russian army took the now familiar route across the Danube and headed towards Constantinople. An equally familiar situation now developed as Britain stepped in to check the Russian advance and, once again, it stopped short of the city on the Bosphorus. By a treaty negotiated early in 1878 an independent state of Bulgaria was created, directly under Russian protection, stretching from the borders of Roumania almost to Constantinople itself. Britain threatened war and Bismarck hastened to intervene. The new Bulgarian state was reduced in size and Nicholas Bunge was left to foot the Russian bill, an important motive in his policy of economic development.

The new ruler of Bulgaria, a German prince, proved an unwilling vassal of the Tsar however and looked to Austria and Germany for support instead. Serbia did the same. Russian agents kidnapped the Bulgarian prince in the early years of Alexander III's reign and forced his abdication, but once again the West intervened and Russia was forced to accept a new

39   A peasant recruit leaves home to join the army

diplomatic defeat. Despite the efforts of both Gorchakov and Bismarck, these crises put a considerable strain upon the League of the Three Emperors. After the first Bismarck concluded a separate alliance with Austria which secretly promised support in the event of an attack by Russia. During the second he published this secret clause. Although he hastened to repair the damage by a treaty of reinsurance with Russia in 1887 the relationship could not be the same again, and early in the next decade the new Emperor of Germany, William I, not only dismissed Bismarck but refused to renew the reinsurance treaty. Towards the end of the reign of Alexander III, therefore, Russia faced a familiar but bitter situation. She stood as far from Constantinople as ever and she was once again isolated in Europe.

One country however had stood aside from the hostile anti-Russian coalition. This was France. France was an old enemy and also a republic, by definition therefore anathema to the Tsar, but diplomacy makes strange bedfellows and Russia began to think in terms of a French alliance to bring them both out of isolation and provide a counterweight to the sinister bloc of the central powers of Europe. The finance ministers provided additional reasons for establishing good relations with France. Russia needed capital for the industrialization programme and the governors of French finance houses, republican and Jewish although they were, could provide these. Diplomacy and gold, therefore, drew the republic and the autocracy together and in July 1891 St Petersburg witnessed a sensational scene. A French naval squadron paid a visit and the Tsar of All the Russias stood bareheaded while the band played the *Marseillaise*. After this military men conferred and in 1894 a formal alliance was concluded between the two states. It was restricted to mutual defence against Germany and Austria. Neither country would support the other in an aggressive war against the central powers and France would give no assistance against Turkey. Nevertheless a diplomatic revolution had taken place, Russia and France had ended a century of hostility and the powers at the ends of Europe were united, at least in the realm of possibilities, against the powers of the centre. From now on mutual suspicions between these blocs were to create an arms race which was ultimately responsible for the First World War and, in Russia's case, for the fall of tsardom. One more change had taken place in the reign of Alexander III which was to have unforeseen and catastrophic consequences in the future.

Like those other events, however, this also lay in the future. Both the

40 Russia's new European policy: Alexander III
(*left*) joins Francis Joseph of Austria–Hungary and
William I of Germany (*right*) in the League of the
Three Emperors

new Tsar, Nicholas II, and Sergius Witte, whose ability rapidly made him a key adviser although the Tsar did not like his Jewish wife and friends, were men in favour of a policy of peace. Nicholas had married, against his father's will, a German princess related to Queen Victoria and the 1890's were a period of good relations between Russia and both Germany and Britain. Francis Joseph, the Emperor of Austria, was also entertained at St Petersburg. Witte was one of the men chiefly responsible for summoning the international conference held at the Hague in 1898 to discuss international methods of keeping peace and reducing armaments. Witte was determined that Russia should not squander her new wealth upon the instruments of war. If Russia must continue to expand, then he pointed her interest in a direction where she might not only reap great material benefits but also avoid an encounter with hostile powers, or so he hoped. He pointed east, into Asia.

41 Count Sergius Witte, Minister of Finance and the architect, more than any other individual, of Russia's industrialization

6 Russia and the East

THE WHOLE OF NORTHERN ASIA exercised an irresistible attraction for Russia's expansionist ambition, to which Peter the Great had been the first to respond. Driving into the Urals in search of iron ore, he had also sent expeditions to trade with China and to explore and annexe the far-off coast of the Pacific. Further south he had despatched ambassadors to test the strength of the surviving Tatar khanates of Khiva and Bukhara and, during the very last years of his reign, himself led an army along the shores of the Caspian Sea to take the cities of Derbent and Baku from the Persian Empire. During the eighteenth century the Asiatic drive lost some of its momentum because Poland and the steppes proved easier and more attractive targets, but with the beginning of the nineteenth the movement was resumed and reached its climax under the influence of Witte.

The first area to attract renewed Russian interest was Georgia. This ancient Christian kingdom, huddled beneath the towering mountains of the Caucasus, had for centuries maintained a precarious independence as a buffer-state between the Persian and Turkish Empires. It was more fortunate than Armenia, an even older Christian state to the west which had fallen to the Turks in the sixteenth century. During the eighteenth century however the last great Persian war-lord, Nadir Shah, set out to conquer Georgia and also took back Derbent and Baku from Russia. King Hercules of Georgia sought the protection of Christian Russia against his Muslim foe. Catherine the Great established a protectorate over Georgia which did not however save the inhabitants of Tiflis from massacre in the closing years of the century. Alexander I announced a formal annexation soon after his accession and the nineteenth-century history of Russia in Asia began. A long contest with both Turkey and Persia, fought in the intervals of the struggle with Napoleon, secured Georgia and recaptured the Caspian coast. Tiflis became the advance base for Russian expansion over the whole area north of the river Aras, where Nicholas I made further conquests.

83

42 The Caucasus: one of Lermontov's own
sketches of this country of rocky defiles and
rushing streams beneath the towering mountains

Between Russia and her new dominions, however, lay the Caucasian
mountain range, an area not unlike the north-west frontier of India and
presenting problems to the Russian advance very similar to those which
the British were encountering in the same period further south. The
routes through the Caucasus were narrow mountain-passes, treacherous
country held by Muslim tribesmen whose friendship was unreliable. The
conquest of the Caucasus became a long and dangerous enterprise which
lasted from the reign of Alexander I into that of Alexander II. Among the
soldiers who fought there was the poet and novelist Michael Lermontov,
whose pages contain vivid descriptions of the wild and beautiful landscape:

A bluish mist was gliding along, escaping from the warm rays of morning as it
poured into the narrow pass nearby; to right and left were mountain ridges,
towering tier upon tier, criss-crossing, long-drawn-out, covered with snowdrifts

and patched with scrub. Far away were these mountains but no two of the crags resembled one another; and all the snows flamed crimson with so gay a colour and looked so bright, that one would have liked to stay and watch for ever. The sun was just peeping from behind the dark blue mountain, which only trained eyes could distinguish from the threatening storm-cloud; but this sun was backed by a blood-red band, to which my fellow-traveller drew my attention.

"I told you", he exclaimed, "that the weather would be bad. We must hurry up if we don't want to leave our bones on Mount Krestovoy."

"Go ahead!" he shouted to the drivers. Leading the horses by the bridle and using the brakes, they began the descent. On the right, the bank rose precipitously; on the left, there was so long and deep a declivity that an Ossete village at the bottom looked like a swallows' nest.[1]

The Ossetes were friendly tribesmen but others were not. The Circassians to the west and the Chechens, Lezghians, and Avars to the east resented the Russian intrusion which threatened to rob them of their ancestral lands. Among the latter, in the eighteen-twenties, a Muslim prophet appeared, named Kazi Mulla, who transformed the defence of the homeland into a Holy War. He was killed in a Russian attack in 1832 but was succeeded by an even more brilliant leader, the Imam Shamil. Against such devout and ferocious opposition the Russian armies faced an unnerving task as they marched through rocky defiles in constant danger not only of the weather but also of avalanche and ambush. The tribesmen left no survivors of their raids. Russian heads bounced and rolled down the mountain-side and Russian hands were nailed to the gates of their fortified villages. During the Crimean war Russian operations were called off completely but finally, between 1857 and 1859, a new expedition forced its way into the fastnesses, clearing forests, building roads and forts, and bombarding the villages with artillery-fire. One by one the tribes lost heart and at length Shamil himself surrendered. He was taken to St Petersburg as an honoured guest of Alexander II and finally allowed to depart for Mecca, the goal of every devout Muslim. At the same time the Circassians gave up resistance and emigrated *en masse* to seek the protection of the Sultan. The Russian conquest of the Caucasus was complete.

Attention now switched further east to the Asian steppes beyond the Caspian and the Tatar khanates of the area known as Turkestan. The nomadic horsemen of the steppes had accepted a vague Russian suzerainty in the eighteenth century because it did not interfere with their livelihood.

[1] Lermontov: *A Hero of Our Own Times*

85

The new Russian drive presented a threat however because it brought settlers to occupy their grazing-lands for arable farming. There was resistance and the Russians suppressed it with military force, employing as their pretext an argument familiar to nineteenth-century imperialists, that it was necessary to secure peace and order along the borders of civilization. Once established on the steppes it was not long before merchants began to covet the settled lands of Turkestan itself. This was prosperous territory, where silk and gold had travelled for centuries along the caravan routes which wound through Tashkent, Bukhara, Khiva, and Samarkand. In the nineteenth century cotton and tobacco crops provided an added attraction. In the reign of Alexander II therefore Russian ambassadors returned to visit the khans and, when their demands for trading concessions were rebuffed, armies followed them. Tashkent, Bukhara, Samarkand, and Khiva fell in turn. At first their rulers were required only to pay heavy reparations for their acts of 'provocation' and to open their markets to Russian trade. By degrees however they lost both their lands and their independence and Turkestan was fully incorporated into the Russian empire. A final Russian thrust brought her armies right to the frontiers of Afghanistan, where they clashed with Afghans in 1885. At this point Britain threatened war in defence of her Indian interests. Bismarck hastened to intervene and the crisis was defused but it became clear that the limits of Russian expansion into central Asia had been reached.

The conquests of the Caucasus and Turkestan compensated Russia for her failure in the Black Sea and the Balkans to some extent. In the last quarter of the century these new territories began to contribute to the Russian industrial revolution. Turkestan supplied raw materials for the textile industry and the Caucasus petroleum. Samarkand was linked to the Caspian by a railway and Baku was linked by rail with Batum, on the Black Sea. The whole was linked to European Russia by the Trans-Caspian railway. The days of colonial wars were over and these distant provinces began to change along with the rest of the empire. The Russification policy was applied and great efforts were made to convert the Muslims to Orthodoxy. Other new forces were also at work. In 1879 Joseph Djugashvili was born of a poor family in a Georgian village. Educated for the old Russia in a seminary for priests at Tiflis, he was expelled for indiscipline in 1899 and became a leading revolutionary agitator among the industrial workers of the new Caucasus under the pseudonym of Stalin. Never a member of Lenin's sophisticated circle in the north, this unpolished and ambitious

86

43 Of coarser grain than Lenin in every respect,
the young Georgian, Stalin, was to prove his equal
in determination and ambition, and to succeed him
in power

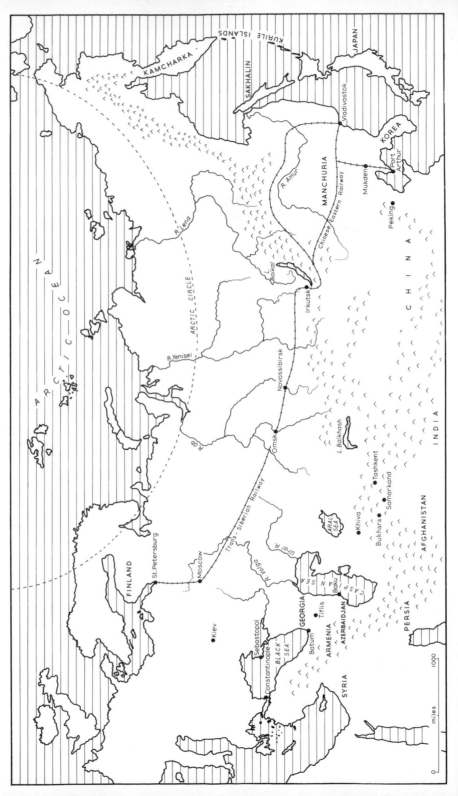

MAP NO. 2 Russian Asia

Georgian was however to become Lenin's successor and rule Communist Russia.

The final direction taken by Russia's Asiatic expansion was across Siberia to the Pacific coast. Since the reign of Peter the Great and, indeed, since the Cossack Yermak freed the routes through the Urals in the sixteenth century, the great Siberian plain had lain open to Muscovite expansion. The rivers Ob and Yenisei and their tributaries, flowing west and east, provided a communications system rather than a natural barrier. Settlers had been relatively few however. Siberia was a hard country, not unlike America west of the Rockies although subjected to a fiercer climate. The plain was covered by thick conifer forest and flooded annually by the rivers. Because of nature's challenge, the men who went to Siberia were tougher and more independent of mind than those who colonized the steppes. Serfdom, as has been seen, was virtually unknown in Siberia, which had been in many ways a freer society than that of Russia as a whole.

For this reason, perhaps, the Tsars were at first reluctant to encourage the development of the east. They sent criminals and political prisoners like Dostoevsky there as a punishment. Speransky was sent to govern eastern Siberia after his disgrace at court. His tidy mind produced an administration and encouraged the enterprise of merchants. Some years later, from 1847–61, he was succeeded as governor by Count Muravyov-Amursky, who proved to be perhaps the first Russian since Peter the Great whose imagination stretched right across the continent to the Pacific and appreciated the full potential of this great tract of land. Muravyov's name incorporated that of the greatest of his conquests, the basin of the river Amur. Since the seventeenth century this river had marked the boundary of Russia to the east. In those days the vigour of the Manchu dynasty of emperors had called a halt to Russian progress but the Chinese Empire, like the Turkish and the Persian, was no longer the power which it once had been. Already, at the beginning of the eighteen-forties, the Manchus had been forced to make trading concessions along the oceanic coast to Britain as the result of the so-called Opium War. Muravyov appreciated the new opportunities open to Russia. In 1849, at his suggestion, Captain Nevelskoy navigated the mouth of the river Amur and demonstrated that this could become Russia's waterway to the Pacific. During the Crimean war soldiers used the route to reinforce Kamchatka, which was held in a fierce but little-known engagement against an Anglo–French naval squadron. The ambitions of the other European powers in China suggested to

Muravyov that Russia might turn the tables upon them in the east. Whereas, in the Turkish Empire, Russia was represented as the aggressor and Britain as the friend of the Sultan, in China there was no doubt that Britain was the enemy to be feared. During the second war between China and the West (1857–60), therefore, Muravyov sailed down the Amur, accompanied it is true by a show of artillery, and argued with the Chinese government that only a Russian alliance could save them from destruction. The Chinese agreed and the Russians were as good as their word. They did not intervene in the hostilities, but through diplomacy persuaded the Western powers not to destroy the Heavenly City of Peking. In return they took for themselves all the territory north of the river Amur and built the port of Vladivostok to play a part comparable to that of St Petersburg in the west as their gateway to the east. The Russo–Chinese agreement also created an understanding between the two empires which was to last for a hundred years, surviving and becoming at first stronger when the Communist revolution in Russia occurred. Not until the century had passed was China in a position to dispute the tsarist gains.

Behind these new frontiers Siberia began to fill with people. Convicts and political exiles remained a staple element in the population, most of them remaining only for as long as they were forced to but contributing something nevertheless to the education and the skills of the territory. At the end of the century however Siberia came into her own. Peasant overpopulation reached a sharp crisis with successive famines and a mass migration, similar in many respects to that which populated the American north-west, began. Since this was Russia, the government followed. Siberia took its place as a full part of the empire. The need to bring it nearer, as it were, to Moscow and St Petersburg for administrative purposes was one of the arguments employed by Sergius Witte to win the Tsar's support for the most ambitious of all his schemes, the construction of a railway from European Russia to the coast of the Pacific. Since he also needed to convince military men within the government, he pointed out the alteration in the balance of power which would follow from a Russian presence in the Far East.

> From the shores of the Pacific and the heights of the Himalayas Russia would dominate not only the affairs of Asia but those of Europe as well.

In truth however Witte himself was unconvinced by this grand but specious argument. His interest in Asia was purely economic. Siberia could solve the peasant problem which was becoming so pressing in western Russia. A trade route to the east would give Russia access to the enormous market of China and the finance of the United States of America.

It was a great vision and the construction of the Trans-Siberian railway was a spectacular engineering achievement. It ran for almost 6,000 miles from Moscow eventually to Vladivostok. Few major obstacles were encountered until the line approached Lake Baikal, where the mountains of central Asia rose to bar the way. The lake was 30 miles wide at its narrowest point and thus impossible to bridge. For some years therefore the railway stopped in the summer at its western edge and passengers crossed by ferry-boat to the opposite side to continue their train-journey. In winter however the lake froze solidly enough to bear the weight of a train running along rails laid across its surface. Eventually a permanent way was constructed from Irkutsk around the southern fringe of the lake and the mountains. At its fullest extent the Trans-Siberian railway offered a journey of nine

44 A locomotive halts at a river-crossing while passengers stretch their legs and break the monotony of the long journey along the Trans-Siberian railway

45 The old and the new combined: the interior
of a travelling church on the Trans-Siberian railway

days from terminus to terminus, the longest railway journey which could
be made in the world without changing trains. In the life of Russian Asia
it played a part similar to those of the great trans-continental railroads in
North America. Villages along its length became towns and minerals,
timber, and grain were transported across the empire. An estimated 200,000
peasants travelled to Siberia each year at the end of the nineteenth century.

The railway thus served Witte's great design for it, and the Russo–
Chinese Bank began to develop his plans for commercial expansion
in the Far East. One immediate advantage of the link with China was that
engineers were able to begin to build the last stretch of the railway, beyond

Lake Baikal, across the northern province of the Chinese Empire known as Manchuria rather than following the much longer route of the Amur basin. After this however Witte's plans ran less smoothly. This was partly because the military men, whose support it had been necessary to enlist, began to interfere in his peaceful programme with strategic projects of their own. Equally responsible however was the interference of a new Far Eastern power, the Empire of Japan.

Japan, until the middle of the nineteenth century, was a picturesque mediaeval society of knights in armour and lotus-blossom. This calm was then shattered by the arrival, in quick succession, of American and Russian fleets requesting the establishment of diplomatic relations and trading privileges. Thus far the picture is the traditional one of imperialism at work. After this however something quite novel occurred. Japan, a society closely knit together by patriotism and loyalty to its semi-divine Emperor, resolved to meet the imperialists upon their own terms. Within forty years the old feudal society had been replaced by growing industries, a modern army and a powerful navy. It was a response quite different from that of China and Russia herself might have learned from it. By the end of the century Japan was ready to play an independent part in the plunder of China and in 1895 acquired, by war, the Liaotung peninsula and Port Arthur. Russia combined with both France and Germany to force the unwelcome interloper to return these gains but, barely three years later and against Witte's advice, Russia acquired Port Arthur for herself and began the construction of a new spur of the Chinese Eastern Railway, as the Manchurian extension of the Trans-Siberian railway was known, to link Port Arthur to the main line of her expansion. Unlike Vladivostok, Port Arthur was ice-free throughout the year. Its acquisition by Russia was thus as important to her eastern plans as the capture of Constantinople would have been in the west. It was an equally dangerous move however. The Western powers were alarmed and Japan determined on revenge.

In 1900 the Boxer Rising occurred in China. This was a limited but fanatical attempt to expel all foreign influence from the empire. The Western powers combined to suppress it and Russia sent forces into Manchuria ostensibly to protect her interests there. Once the rising was over however she declined to withdraw them. Japan protested and Russia finally agreed·to evacuate the area within the next couple of years. Meanwhile Japan and Britain concluded a treaty of mutual defence. Clearly a dangerous tension was arising and Witte urged Russia not to run the risk

93

46 As the state mobilized for the Russo-Japanese
war, scenes familiar to tsarist Russia were enacted
yet again as conscription divided tearful and
bewildered families

of losing all her gains by a ruinous war. Never popular with the new Tsar,
Nicholas II, he was now removed from office by the efforts of his rivals
and the situation slid rapidly out of control. The minister of the interior
even remarked that 'a small but successful war' might prove useful to the
régime by restoring the loyalty of the country to the Tsar. The troops were
not withdrawn from Manchuria by the stipulated date and Japan declared
war.

Since Japan was the aggressor, Britain was relieved of an obligation to
intervene. Russia's ally, France, made last-minute efforts to keep the peace
but was prepared to go no further than that. The Russo–Japanese war thus
became a straightforward contest between the old empire and the new and
speedily revealed that Russia was as incapable of meeting the new challenge
as she had been to resist the great powers of the West. Japanese destroyers

made a surprise attack upon Port Arthur and, although they inflicted no decisive damage, established a blockade which the Russian fleet could not break. Returning from one vain sortie the flagship of Admiral Makarov was blown up by a mine in the harbour entrance and the admiral and almost all his crew were killed. Meanwhile a Japanese army advanced into the Liaotung peninsula and put Port Arthur under siege from the landward side.

With the Pacific fleet bottled up in Port Arthur, the Russian high command took a decision more foolhardy than any so far described in this history. This was to send the Baltic fleet half way round the world to relieve the siege. The fleet departed in the full panoply of tradition. The Tsar toured the ships and blessed them before they sailed and orders were given for the guns and decks to be sprinkled with holy water before they went into action. More practical considerations were however lacking. The ships were ill-founded and rusty, the officers inexperienced aristocrats and the seamen peasants in uniform. In a North Sea fog the formation encountered a British trawler-fleet on the Dogger Bank and the supply-ship *Kamchatka* signalled that she was being pursued by torpedo-boats. In a panic the Russian battleships opened fire for twenty minutes. Only when the fog had cleared and they were celebrating their first victory did they discover

47 'The Russian Octopus': a Japanese cartoon expresses Japan's view of Russia's expansion into Asia

48 With the Pacific Fleet bottled up at
Port Arthur, the dubiously efficient

Baltic Fleet embarks for its ill-fated
voyage around the world

the identity of their assailants and learn that they had brought Russia and Britain within sight of war.

French diplomacy intervened however and the Russian fleet was merely shadowed on its way through the English Channel. All British home and colonial ports were closed to it and the officer in command, Admiral Rozhestvensky, decided to lead his ships around Africa via the French colonial ports rather than past Gibraltar and through the Suez Canal. This plan entailed long hauls between scattered and fever-ridden tropical ports. Shortage of coal reduced speed, there were many desertions at the occasional landfalls, disease broke out upon the ships and finally mutiny. In April 1905 the fleet limped into Kamrang Bay in the South China Sea unfit to do anything but wait for a month to refit and recover.

49   In a desperate attempt to halt the Japanese advance on Port Arthur, the Russian army destroyed its own rail communications in Manchuria

Meanwhile Port Arthur had fallen after a siege of 156 days and Russia had lost all hope of recovering it from the landward side. At Mukden, a crucial link on the railway, Russian and Japanese armies engaged for three weeks in winter mud and inflicted enormous losses upon each other. Finally the Russians withdrew to the north and abandoned the port to its fate. Not without heroism, Rozhestvensky decided to make a desperate attempt to redeem the situation. His crippled fleet steamed into the Tsushima Straits to challenge the Japanese Admiral Togo and within twenty minutes had been destroyed. Twenty-three ships were sunk, some captured and only four eventually reached Vladivostok. 4,830 Russian sailors lost their lives and 110 Japanese. The short but disastrous war ended with the Treaty of Portsmouth (U.S.A.), signed in August. Japan took the peninsula, the

50   As discontent grows, a Guards officer has to run for his life in a working-class district of St Petersburg

railway, and Port Arthur. Her occupation of Korea was confirmed. Russia was pushed back again to the River Amur.

Ironically, Russia's negotiator at Portsmouth was Sergius Witte. The statesman who had planned to compensate his country for her reverses in the west by a new programme of economic and commercial expansion in the east was called on to witness a renewed defeat for Russian arms and the collapse of most of his great design. As before in history, Russian soldiers had fought with sacrificial bravery but with the familiar poor leadership and inadequate planning and equipment of earlier wars. As in the past, moreover, a defeat abroad produced a crisis at home. So far from strengthening the Tsar's prestige, the Russo–Japanese war destroyed it at a crucially important moment when he required all the loyalty from his armed forces and his people which he could command. Internally, Russia was on the brink of revolution and her defeat in Asia served to push her over the edge.

7 The Last Tsar and the First Revolution

NICHOLAS ROMANOV was born in 1868; Vladimir Ulyanov in 1870. The last Tsar and the founder of Communist Russia were thus almost exact contemporaries but here any resemblance between them ends. In 1894, when Nicholas began to reign, Ulyanov was practising as a barrister in St Petersburg and setting out upon the revolutionary career which was to make him famous under the pseudonym of Lenin. In 1896, when Nicholas was crowned, he was in prison, writing pamphlets using milk as ink and inkwells made of bread and shortly to begin a three-year exile in Siberia. Nicholas was a short and insignificant man, mild-mannered, affable, and shy. Lenin was a man of striking appearance with brilliant eyes and a huge, domed forehead which indicated his intellectual power. Men who heard him compared his voice in argument to a hammer or a drill, harsh, insistent, and remorseless. Nicholas was a devoted family man dominated by his wife, the German princess Alexandra. Lenin's wife, Nadia Krupskaya, waited outside her husband's prison and accompanied him into exile as his devoted partner and supporter.

Weak and indecisive though he was in so many ways, the Tsar was stubborn. 'Let every man know,' he said at the outset of his reign, 'that I will devote all of my strength to the good of my people, but that I will uphold the principle of the autocracy as firmly and as unflinchingly as did my ever-lamented father.'

In the situation which he inherited and which continued to develop during his reign this combination of qualities proved fatal. Lenin, although arrogant and intolerant of opposition, was always ready to learn from experience. While Nicholas squandered his opportunities to save tsardom, he exploited every chance which fortune and the Tsar's mistakes offered to advance the cause of revolution. Eventually the Tsar lost both his throne and his life. The son of a schools-inspector became the new ruler of the Russian Empire.

From the outset of his political career Lenin rejected both the terrorist tactics which had led to his brother's death and the Populist tradition which put its faith in the Russian peasants as the agents of revolution. With Plekhanov, he was among the founders of the Russian Social Democratic Labour Party in 1898, a Marxist movement which directed its agitation to the proletariat of the industrial towns. Even this movement, Lenin was convinced, must possess a different structure to political parties of the Left elsewhere. Russia possessed no parliament and only a weak and persecuted trade union movement. On the other hand the tsarist state and its political police force were among the strongest in Europe. A Socialist or trade union party like those of western Europe, therefore, aiming at parliamentary representation and peaceful reform, was out of the question. The party must be revolutionary and it must also operate in secret. A tight and well-disciplined organization was also essential, Lenin argued:

> broad democracy in Party organization, amidst the gloom of autocracy and the domination of gendarme selection, is nothing more than a useless and harmful toy. . . . because any attempt to practise broad democratic principles will simply facilitate the work of the police in making big raids, it will perpetuate the prevailing primitiveness, divert the thoughts of the practical workers from the serious and imperative task of training themselves to become revolutionaries to that of drawing up detailed paper rules for election systems.

By definition, therefore, Lenin's 'party of a new type' was a small organization. When it took the title of Bolsheviks, or majority men, this was a purely propagandist move, because most of the Social Democrats disliked both the idea of abandoning their hopes for a Russian parliament and the dictatorial leadership by Lenin and his associates which his arguments implied. His new party seemed even less significant by comparison with the Social Revolutionaries, founded in 1902 to continue the work of the Populists among the peasants who formed the vast majority of the working population of Russia. At first Lenin's tactics and his exclusiveness made the Bolsheviks a weak force in Russian politics. Lenin himself was absent from St Petersburg, in self-imposed exile beyond the reach of the law, when both the revolutions of 1905 and 1917 began. Eventually however his tactics were vindicated. Because the Bolsheviks were organized and disciplined they retained their freedom of action in periods of revolutionary chaos. Although Lenin never lost sight of his ultimate goal he was able to modify his tactics according to the rapid and, to others, bewildering, shifts in the course of events. The Mensheviks, as the more moderate wing of the

51 The Ulyanov family in 1879: Vladimir, later to be known as Lenin, is seated on the extreme right. His brother Alexander, hanged in 1887 for his part in a plot against the Tsar, is standing at the back

Social Democratic party became known, and the Social Revolutionaries failed to gain power and were relegated, in the vivid phrase of the Bolshevik Trotsky, to 'the rubbish-heap of history'. The Bolsheviks succeeded to the empire of the Tsars.

The tide of revolution rose steadily throughout the first ten years of Nicholas's reign. Even his coronation day was marred by violence. A huge crowd assembled for the traditional distribution of gifts by a new Tsar. When he appeared they rushed forward through barriers and across a field full of ditches, dug to hold them back. Thousands fell and were crushed by the mob behind them. Before the police could restore order over 1,000 had been killed and 500 injured. Accidental though this tragedy

52 The reign of the last Tsar opened with a
tragedy, as thousands of peasants were trampled
to death in wild scenes at the coronation of Nicholas
II and Alexandra

seems clearly to have been, radical students chose to make it the pretext
for a demonstration at the cemetery where the victims were buried. Three
years later, student demonstrators in the streets of St Petersburg were
charged by mounted police. They declared a strike to which the authorities
replied by expelling political activists and conscripting them into the
armed forces. Such incidents were perhaps only the froth on the surface
of politics but they reflected and also contributed to a discontent which
ran deeper. In the countryside the plight of the peasants was slowly becoming desperate. Although the amount of land which they occupied had
increased considerably since emancipation, one peasant in three remained
landless and the average size of a holding had decreased by one-third.
Many tenants paid as much as half their crop to a landlord in return for a

few acres of land. Established farmers remained subject to redemption payments and the interference of the commune. All classes in the countryside
suffered under the taxes on consumer goods. In the 1890s, successive years
of famine brought these accumulated grievances to a critical pitch. Sergius
Witte's Siberian policy proved only a palliative, not an antidote to the
situation and at the turn of the century riots and disturbances became
increasingly frequent. Reactionaries at court blamed the minister for
disturbing the peace of the countryside and this was the chief reason
for his dismissal. Nicholas himself in any case disliked him for his Jewish
connections.

In the towns working and living conditions provided fertile ground for
the seeds of Socialist agitation. Strikes became frequent and once again the
Cossacks and the mounted police seemed the régime's only answers.
Plehve, the Minister of the Interior who had served since the reign of
Alexander III and who had supported the far eastern policy which he
thought might lead to a 'small but successful war', was assassinated by a
Social Revolutionary in July 1904. His successor, Sviatopolk-Mirsky, made
one concession to radical demands by allowing a national conference of
zemstvo leaders to meet in the capital. This served only to increase the
excitement for the conference proceeded to demand far-reaching reforms
in the countryside and the calling of a parliament. While Socialists sold the
Bolshevik newspaper *The Spark* in factories and spoke at street-corners
with one eye constantly looking for the approach of the police, aristocratic
and middle-class liberals met in greater comfort at political banquets remi-
niscent of those which in Paris had preceded the fall of Louis Philippe in
1848. At the beginning of 1905, therefore, when news of the far eastern
disasters began to reach St Petersburg, all the ingredients of revolution were
present. On the afternoon of Sunday, 9 January, a great demonstration
took place in the capital. The government, in one shrewd attempt to head
off working-class unrest, had permitted the formation of a trade union,
the Assembly of Russian Factory Workers. It was closely supervised by the
police and led, with a characteristically tsarist touch, by a priest, Father
George Gapon. It was Gapon who now led a huge but orderly crowd to the
Winter Palace with a petition asking for an eight-hour day, a minimum wage
and a parliament. The great procession of men, women, and children
carried holy ikons and pictures of the Tsar and, when it reached the square
before the palace, knelt in the snow to sing the national anthem. The Tsar
was at his country residence however and in his absence the police and

53 'Bloody Sunday' in St Petersburg: in the
Tsar's absence the Guards at the Winter Palace
shoot down the peaceful demonstrators

military authorities ordered the crowd to disperse. Then, without further
warning, they opened fire upon the packed and motionless crowd. Hundreds
were killed, more in the panic which ensued.

'Bloody Sunday', as it soon became known, was the spark to the bonfire
which now engulfed Russia. New strikes broke out and riots quite different
in character from that peaceful demonstration. Grand Duke Sergius,

governor of Moscow, was assassinated. New peasant riots convulsed the
countryside and nationalist risings took place in Poland, the Baltic States,
the Ukraine, and the Caucasus. The universities rose again and, most significantly for the future of tsardom, there were mutinies in the armed forces.
The least important but the most spectacular of these occurred at Odessa,
where the crew of the battleship *Potemkin* put to sea and repelled attacks
by other Russian warships for several days before sailing into a Roumanian
port to surrender. The defeat in the Far East had done its work however in
spreading disaffection among soldiers and sailors. Nicholas' prestige had

54   Ordered to eat rotten cabbage soup, and to be
shot when they refused to do so, the crew of the

sunk very low and he could not call upon the last resort of tsardom, armed
force, with any confidence that it would come to his aid.

The Tsar himself was not a bloodthirsty man. He had been horrified to
hear the news of Bloody Sunday and had personally created a fund for the
relatives and dependents of the victims. In the crisis of authority which
followed his first thought was for the re-establishment of law and order
however and he contemplated placing the whole empire under martial
law. When it became clear that this was impossible, for the reasons just
explained, he came reluctantly to the conclusion that he must meet at least
some of the people's demands. In making this decision he was assisted by
Witte, whose return to power had been one of the few good results of the

Potemkin mutinied and sailed the Black Sea until forced
by shortages of food, coal, and fresh water to surrender

Russo–Japanese war. Witte was no democrat but he realized that only the
promise of a parliament could save the monarchy. In October therefore,
while St Petersburg was paralyzed by a general strike, a manifesto was
issued in the Tsar's name undertaking to summon a State Duma and

> to establish as an unchangeable principle that no law can obtain force without
> the consent of the State Duma and that to the elected of the people there should
> be granted the possibility of actual participation in supervision of the legality
> of the actions of the authorities appointed by Us.

The effect of this proclamation was a remarkable tribute to Witte's shrewd-
ness. It immediately divided moderates from extremists and siphoned off

most of the political excitement into an election campaign. It revealed that there had been no co-ordination behind the widespread demonstrations. There was a world of difference between banqueting liberals and street-corner socialists and between the capital and the provinces. St Petersburg and Moscow had produced the only elements of organization in the revolution – Soviets or councils of strike committees. When the October Manifesto was issued the strikes in the cities had ended and when the Soviets attempted to renew them they discovered that they had become isolated. Even the soldiers' loyalty had returned and the strikers were cleared from the streets by artillery fire. Punitive columns set out for the provinces.

Only Lenin seems fully to have realized that the revolution was over. From his exile he ordered the Bolsheviks to play no part in the election campaign, partly no doubt because their numbers and following were too small to make much of a showing but chiefly because he suspected that the parliament would achieve nothing. The remaining parties gave their whole energy to the task however. The Lower House of the Duma was to be elected on a universal manhood franchise and they saw this, in their excitement, as the beginning of a new age in Russia. When the first Russian parliament assembled in April 1906, almost one hundred years after Speransky had first sketched its constitution, it was full of men bursting with the confidence of their convictions, even though the differences among their policies remained as great as ever. Social Revolutionaries made up almost a quarter of the membership of the Lower House. The zemstvo radicals, calling themselves the Constitutional Democrats or Cadets, reaped the harvest of half a century of political activity in the provinces by occupying half the seats. They now demanded a redistribution of the land, an income-tax levied upon all classes, and workers' health insurance financed by a levy upon employers. The Octobrists were a more moderate party, representing business interests in the cities and by definition therefore few in number. Loyal monarchists were even fewer. Social Democrats who had ignored Lenin's wishes and succeeded in winning election were similarly few. The overall political complexion was however quite clearly left of centre. Despite its internal divisions the First Duma was a body which would demand radical reform.

In fact its political colouring doomed the First Duma to extinction from the start. The Tsar had enfranchised the peasants relying upon their traditional loyalty to redress the extremism of the cities. When it became clear that this stratagem had not succeeded he had no further use for their

55 Peasant Deputies arrive at the Duma as Russia
takes her first steps towards parliamentary
democracy

representatives. The October Manifesto moreover had made no promise of
legislative powers, only a degree of consultation. The members of the
Lower House now learned that their reform proposals were 'inadmissible'.
They retained a veto over taxation but this was not to extend either to military or naval estimates or to the expenditure of the royal household. The
ministers would continue to be appointed by the Tsar and responsible to
him alone. They were not even obliged to give full replies to parliamentary
questions. The speaker had a right of audience with the Tsar but he was to
be the only avenue of communication. For two months therefore the Tsar
and the Duma faced each other with mutual suspicion and impatience.
Finally the radical members played what they regarded as their master-
card. The government's impending bankruptcy as a result of the Russo–
Japanese war had been one of the most powerful motives impelling Witte

56 Chosen as the 'strong man' who could end peasant unrest, Peter Stolypin made enemies on every side by his uncompromising methods and was mysteriously assassinated

to summon the Duma. They now called upon the people not to pay taxes until the Tsar acceded to their demands. Witte had already trumped their ace however. During the winter he had negotiated a huge French loan which left Nicholas free to dispense both with him and the Duma. The people did not respond to the radical demand and soldiers occupied the palace where the assembly met and forcibly dissolved it. A group of left-wing members went to Finland and issued a new manifesto but this resulted only in their own arrest.

Thus Russia's first modern parliament ended almost as soon as it had begun. It was not the last however, although the Second Duma, summoned in 1907, proved to contain more leftists than the first and was dismissed almost as quickly. After this the Tsar's new chief minister, Peter Stolypin, drastically revised the voting laws to reduce lower-class and non-Russian influence and the Third Duma, summoned in the autumn of 1907, produced in consequence a solid basis of Octobrists and right-wing monarchists. Because of this and because the Tsar soon needed renewed financial support this Duma ran its five-year course until 1912 and was succeeded by another, similarly composed, which lasted until 1917. The history of these Russian parliaments is very similar to that of the English parliaments of James I and Charles I, in the seventeenth century. In each case the monarch summoned the assembly only as the last resort of political or financial necessity. In each case he and his ministers made great efforts to 'pack' its benches with loyalists and dismissed it when conflict arose or when he could escape from its purse-strings. With the exception of Stolypin, Nicholas's ministers ignored the Duma as often as they could. Although, as time passed, they were forced to grant it increased powers of legislation, (the Duma itself was responsible for introducing only 34 out of over 2,000 bills enacted during this period. These were chiefly concerned with education and agriculture. The Speaker of the later Dumas, Michael Rodzyanko, left in his memoirs a bitter record of the frustrations which he encountered in dealing with the Tsar, who constantly accused the Duma of interfering with his autocratic powers. Nevertheless the Duma survived and, given time, it might have emerged from its early trials to acquire a prestige and a power comparable to the English parliament. In England however, it must be remembered, parliament had won its final position only after dethroning two kings. Perhaps a similar development in Russia was also inevitable. Nicholas did not trust the Duma and Lenin was constantly at work trying to undermine its authority among the people. The result of this was that Russia, when her second revolution came, followed a path which once again diverged from that of the West. The Tsar was deposed but the infant parliament quickly followed him into oblivion. The four Dumas of 1906–17 were not only the first parliaments in Russian history but also the last.

Peter Stolypin, who followed Witte, was a landowner and former provincial governor. Unlike Witte he put the peasants first in his programme. It was certainly time to do so, but Stolypin quickly gained a bad reputation among radicals for both his methods and his aims. Under him the flickering peasant unrest was suppressed by martial law. Thousands of trouble-makers were arrested and given summary trial. Many were executed within twenty-four hours of their sentence and gallows festooned the countryside. In his plans for a better future Stolypin contradicted both the sweeping idealism

57   A devoted family man, Nicholas II was happiest
in the company of his children. Here he stands with
his unfortunate son and heir, his second daughter,
the Grand Duchess Tatiana, and Prince Nikita

of the Cadets, who wished to break up estates and farms into still smaller units so that every peasant might have his few acres, and the communistic programme of the Socialists. He preferred, in his own phrase, 'to take account of the sound and the strong, not the drunken and the weak'. He aimed to help that minority of peasants who were prepared to help themselves. By doing this, he argued, a vigorous class of enterprising farmers would be created which would revitalize Russian agriculture and at the same time provide a solidly loyalist vote in the countryside. In order to achieve this Stolypin struck off the shackles of the commune. The peasant was empowered by law to consolidate his strips of land and hold his farm permanently, without fear of redistribution. The government would carry out the necessary surveys and advance the capital required. The new farmer became personally responsible for his taxes. Communes in which there had been no redistribution since 1861 were abolished.

These steps marked the beginning of an agricultural revolution in Russia just as surely as Witte's policies had laid the foundations of industrial change. Within a few years official records counted well over a million *kulaks*, or independent peasant farmers, living on newly consolidated farms, employing new agricultural methods and constantly increasing productivity. What might have happened next however belongs once again to the realm of the imponderable. War, revolution, and civil war crippled Russian agriculture in the next few years and the victorious Communists set out systematically to destroy the kulak class. Stolypin himself was no more fortunate. His house had been blown up and his daughter seriously injured at the outset of his period of office. In 1911 he accompanied the Tsar on a visit to Kiev and there, in a box at the Opera, he was shot and mortally wounded by a revolutionary terrorist.

'He is gone; let us hear no more of him' said Alexandra when she heard the news. Almost wilfully the monarchy seemed to disown its ablest servants. The Tsarina's favourite was a very different type of man. Gregory Rasputin was an illiterate Siberian peasant who had deserted his family and wandered the countryside collecting followers by his claim to holiness and supernatural powers. This type of person, known as a *starets*, was familiar in Russian history but hitherto unknown at the court of St Petersburg, unless the legend of Alexander I is to be entertained. Rasputin had been introduced there in 1905 however and soon became a favourite. Nicholas regarded him as his own special link with the people, an authentic and simple Russian among the shifty intellectuals and intriguers of the

58 Gregory Rasputin, the sinister self-styled holy
man, among the ladies of the Court in St
Petersburg

political scene. Alexandra venerated him as a man of God. The heir to the
throne, Alexander, was the Tsar's only son. He was a frail and sickly boy,
cursed by the disease of haemophilia. The effect of this ailment is that any
cut or bruise is likely to set up an internal bleeding which cannot be
staunched, since the blood will not clot. Rasputin seemed able to cure this
condition however merely by talking to the boy. His powers of hypnosis
may have been the secret of his uncanny success but, whatever the medical
explanation, the Tsarina believed that he had been sent from God by a
miracle to preserve the Romanov line.

Elsewhere in the court Rasputin was cordially hated, both for his low
birth and for his personal habits. He was ignorant and filthy, a heavy
drinker and a lustful man who did not confine his appetites to gipsies and
prostitutes but pressed his attentions, with considerable success, upon
the ladies of the court. Even the phlegmatic Stolypin testified to the power
of his personality:

116

He ran his pale eyes over me, mumbled mysterious and inarticulate words from the Scriptures, made strange movements with his hands, and I began to feel an indescribable loathing for this vermin sitting opposite me. Still, I did realize that the man possessed great hypnotic power, which was beginning to produce a strong moral impression on me, though certainly one of repulsion. I pulled myself together, and addressing him roughly, told him that on the strength of the evidence in my possession I could annihilate him by prosecuting him as a sectarian. I then ordered him to leave St Petersburg immediately of his own free will for his native village and never show his face here again.

Stolypin was assassinated however and Rasputin was brought back to court by a lady of the Tsarina's entourage. Renewed attempts to discredit and remove him all failed. He began to be accused of exercising political influence. The Duma in particular detested him on this account and held him chiefly responsible for the Tsar's refusal to accept its advice.

The evidence is vague and inconclusive at this stage. The corrupt holy man was probably a symptom of what was wrong at court rather than a cause. His presence and his reputation however cast a strange and revealing light over Russia on the eve of the First World War. The sharp contrasts which had always characterized the history of the country had never appeared more bizarre and enigmatic. On the one hand Russia was undergoing an industrial and agrarian revolution, breaking loose from its medieval shackles and beginning to develop the forms of a modern society and a constitutional government. On the other its highest politics were pervaded by the dim religious mysticism of the distant past. St Petersburg was a sophisticated European city, famous throughout Europe for its art treasures and the glories of the Imperial Ballet. Through its streets and palaces however flitted the incongruous figure of an unkempt religious crook, while beyond the boulevards simmered another world of slum housing, industrial discontent and revolutionary agitation. Still trapped halfway between the future and the past, Imperial Russia now deliberately took the steps which led to the First World War and the final crisis of tsardom.

8 The End of Tsardom

RUSSIA BECAME INVOLVED in the First World War because of the age-old and fatal fascination of Constantinople and the Balkans. For almost twenty years this interest had lain dormant while the Tsar pursued the new policy in the Far East. Both Austria and Russia had agreed to maintain the Ottoman Empire in existence and Russia had turned a deaf ear and a blind eye to Turkish massacres of Armenians and Macedonians. The disaster of the Russo–Japanese war strengthened the need for good relations with the West and in 1907 Russia reached agreement with Britain over both the Turkish Empire and their mutual frontiers in central Asia. In 1908 however events took a fresh turn and the Turkish question was re-opened. In eastern Europe, just as everywhere else in the continent at this period, a strident and aggressive nationalism took possession of both rulers and peoples. King Peter Karageorgovich of Serbia dreamed of extending the frontiers of his tiny state to include all the western Slavs and particularly those at present living in Austrian-occupied Bosnia and Herzegovina. Bulgaria contemplated a similar expansion further east. Finally the wave of national feeling swept into Turkey itself. The Young Turks, a movement composed of army officers and admirers of the West, demanded an end to the old policy of subservience to the powers. They deposed the last Sultan, Abdul Hamid, and set about a policy of wide-ranging reform.

These events had an inevitable sequel within Russia. A wave of Pan-Slav excitement rolled through the cities and demanded support for the Serbs and the Bulgars. The Turkish revolution seemed to add a further note of urgency. If the Sick Man of Europe were to recover his vitality then the Straits might be lost forever. Both the Tsar and his ministers however realized that prudence was essential. Russia remained militarily weak and could not afford the risk of war. It was clear that Austria was determined not to lose ground to Serbia and Germany was actively supporting the Young Turks. The foreign minister, Isvolsky, proceeded therefore with the caution of his nineteenth-century predecessors. Preferring the slightly

59 Tsar Nicholas II (*centre*) with the King and
Crown Prince of Roumania at Constanza in 1910

more concrete prospect of the Straits to the dubious attractions of a Slav crusade, he met his Austrian counterpart, Baron Aehrenthal, in September 1908 and negotiated a new agreement. Russia might re-open the question of the Straits for discussion among the powers. Austria, in return, might formally annexe Bosnia and Herzegovina. This seemed to be a success for Russian diplomacy, albeit a limited one, but before Isvolsky could begin his delicate task Aehrenthal declared the annexation and left Russia stranded. In a fury, the duped Isvolsky pledged Russian support for Serbia against the aggressor but this sudden switch of policy produced only further disaster. Germany promised to support Austria to the point of war, if necessary. France would make no such commitment to Russia. Russia had been outmanœuvred and isolated once again, not a new experience but no less galling for that. For the moment however she could do nothing but climb down.

This was not to be the end of the affair however. Within the Balkans everything was now in motion. Serbian agents became active in Bosnia, enlisting enthusiastic students in plots for assassination and revolt against the Austrian overlords. Further east, Serbia and Bulgaria joined forces with Greece and Montenegro in 1912 and declared war on Turkey, swiftly over-running the whole of Macedonia. Early in 1913 the Bulgarian war hero Radko Dmitriev went to Moscow 'on a secret mission', in his own words, 'to lay Constantinople at his Majesty's feet.' Public enthusiasm, in which the Duma joined, was hysterical, but the government once again drew back. The great powers intervened in the Balkans, a conference was called in London and the ambitions of both Serbia and Bulgaria were checked. The Balkan states now fell out among themselves over their respective shares of the much-reduced spoils and in the new war which resulted Turkey was able to recover some of her lost ground.

This was how affairs stood in the Balkans on 28 June 1914, when a Bosnian student named Gavrilo Prinzip fired the shots at Sarajevo which killed Archduke Francis Ferdinand, the heir to the Austrian throne, and Sophie his wife. Almost a month later Vienna despatched an ultimatum to Belgrade demanding humiliating apologies and the admission of Austrian police to Serbia to hunt the killers. The demands were so arrogant and insulting as to constitute an invitation to refuse them. Austria had used the intervening weeks to consult with her German ally and receive a pledge of uncompromising support. She was searching for a pretext to overrun Serbia and clip the wings of her ambition. Against all expectations

MAP NO. 3
Constantinople and the Balkans

60 When Russia entered the First World War,
Nicholas assumed the traditional role of a

however the Serbs accepted most of the demands. Austria pressed on and
declared war on 28 July.

Russia was plunged into a crisis of confidence. It was her advice which
had persuaded the Serbs not to resist the Austrian demands. To stand back
now that war had been declared would be a third betrayal of the Slav cause
within a few years. Russia's prestige in the Balkans and her ambition for
the Straits would surely both be lost for the foreseeable future. To support
Serbia however would almost certainly bring war. On 29 July Germany
warned that 'further continuation of Russian mobilization would force us
to mobilize also'. The mobilization of an army was a slow and deliberate
process, slower in Russia than anywhere else in Europe and certainly
slower than in Germany. Russia must either act or unconditionally surrender

Tsar, riding to lead his soldiers in person and giving
them his blessing with a holy ikon in his hand

the Serbs to their fate. In this crisis the Tsar hesitated and at one stage
ordered a halt to mobilization. His Ministers and the Duma pushed him
on however. Russian mobilization continued and on 1 August Germany
declared war. On 3 August she declared war on Russia's western ally
France, anxious to gain the advantage of striking the first blow in a two-
front war which seemed inevitable. On 4 August Britain declared war on
Germany when German armies violated the neutrality of Belgium in their
advance upon France. Four days of diplomatic bluff and counter-bluff
thus caused a war which lasted for four years and inflicted catastrophe upon
all those who took part in it. It seems idle to apportion blame for its outbreak and Nicholas perhaps deserves sympathy in his dilemma. His fears
for the outcome were well-founded, perhaps better-founded than he

realized. The clear-sighted Lenin had written from exile in 1913 that

> a war between Austria and Russia would be a very useful thing for the revolution, but it is not likely that Francis Joseph and Nikolasha will give us this pleasure.

Against his better judgment however Nicholas had obliged and from the war emerged the revolution which gave Lenin his opportunity.

Ironically however, the first effect of the declaration of war was a great outburst of Russian loyalty to the Tsar. When he appeared, with Alexandra, on the balcony of the Winter Palace,

> a vast crowd filled the whole square and all the adjacent streets. At the sight of the Emperor, an electric current seemed to pass through the mass of people; a mighty 'hurrah' filled the air. Banners and placards, on which were inscribed the words "Long live Russia and the Slavonic cause", were lowered to the ground, and the whole crowd, as one man, fell on their knees before the Emperor. He tried to speak, raised his hand: the front rows endeavoured to silence the rest but nothing could be heard amid the deafening cheers and roaring of the crowd. The Emperor stood for a while with bowed head, overpowered by the solemnity of the moment, when Tsar and people became one. Then he turned slowly, and withdrew into his apartments.

It was a traditional scene, utterly different from those which the same square had witnessed nine years before and also from those which it was to see enacted less than three years later. For the moment thoughts of revolution were forgotten. According to the same eye-witness, the President of the Duma,

> on leaving the palace we mingled with the crowd of demonstrators, and came across some factory workers, I stopped them and asked how they came to be here, when they had been on strike, and almost on the point of an armed rising a short time ago. The workmen replied: "That was our own family dispute. We thought reforms came too slowly through the Duma. But now all Russia is involved. We have rallied to our Tsar as to our emblem, and we shall follow him for the sake of victory over the Germans."

Almost equally surprisingly, the war began with victories for Russian arms. The bulk of Germany's forces were concentrated on the French front and the Russians advanced rapidly into East Prussia on either side of the Masurian Lakes. The First Army routed a German force at Gumbinnen and caused the panic withdrawal of forces from the west, a step which slowed the German advance in that direction and was probably decisive in lengthening a war which everyone had expected to be over quickly into the long conflict of attrition which the First World War became. The

Russians paid for their success with massive defeats in the next few months however. 150,000 Russian soldiers were taken prisoner at the battles of Tannenberg and the Masurian Lakes. In 1915 the Germans advanced into Galicia and captured more prisoners, Warsaw, and most of Lithuania. Turkey had joined the Central Powers and the Straits were lost. In a desperate reversal of the policy of a century, Britain agreed to a Russian occupation of the Straits and sent a military and naval force to capture them. At Gallipoli and the Dardanelles this strategy failed completely. Bulgaria joined the Central Powers. Serbia was overrun.

This rapid conversion of victory into defeat took place against a background of rapidly mounting chaos within Russia, which proved once again incapable of mounting a war effort on the home front. Goods trains arrived in Moscow packed with wounded men who lay on the wooden floors of the trucks without clothes, food, or proper dressings for their wounds. Military supplies for the fighting troops were no better. Rifles, boots, and ammunition were all in equally short supply. The loss of the Straits had closed the main route by which allied supplies could reach Russia or Russian exports reach the West. The land was stripped of peasants by conscription. Bread supplies failed in the towns and there were riots. Monetary inflation far outpaced the rise in wages in the war industries. To some extent these failures could be blamed upon the bureaucracy and unscrupulous war-profiteers, just as the military defeats could be blamed upon commanders. Late in 1915 Nicholas himself decided to take command at the front however and his own prestige began to suffer by association with defeat. He left behind a government in which Russia saw four prime ministers, six ministers of the interior, three ministers of foreign affairs, and six of defence within two years. The Duma and the zemstvos did what they could to organize medical supplies and munitions. A Central War Industries Committee was created in St Petersburg, now renamed Petrograd in a patriotic Slavonic style instead of the German, to deal with the wartime emergencies of production. In order to encourage the workers' participation in the war effort representatives of the factories were elected to this body along with those of employers and members of the Duma.

Despite these efforts at national solidarity, however, distrust continued to fester between the people's representatives and those of the distant Tsar. In particular patriots claimed to discern behind the succession of futile ministers who came and went the disruptive influence of the Tsarina and Rasputin. Alexandra's German blood made her doubly unpopular and

61   Petrograd 1917: the bread-lines form, and soon
patience will give way to anger and revolution

Rasputin was widely believed to be in the pay of German agents. Late in 1916 a group of aristocratic conspirators led by Prince Felix Yusopov planned to assassinate him. They lured him to an assignation in a cellar with promises of wine and women and plied him with drugged wine and poisoned cakes. These failed to kill him however and in a macabre scene he was shot at close range several times before he fell in the snow while trying to escape. His body was wrapped in a curtain and bundled into the freezing waters of the river Neva. Like all the assassinations in Russian history this one solved nothing. More than one man's death was required to end the millions of deaths being inflicted at the front, and more than patriotism was needed to reverse the tide of inefficiency and defeat. Indeed patriotism itself was waning rapidly among both the ill-equipped soldiers at the front and the hungry masses at home. In 1916 General Brusilov made a dramatic breakthrough in Galicia and advanced 150 miles but this was small compensation to Russia for the thousands of deserters who, in Lenin's vivid phrase, were 'voting with their feet' against the war and the Tsar. When new efforts were made to recruit men in the Asiatic provinces a widespread revolt broke out.

In Petrograd the year 1917 opened on a depressing scene. The winter weather was as bitter as ever and long queues waited outside baker's shops which seldom opened. On the anniversary of Bloody Sunday strikes occurred and the worker members of the Central War Industries Committee were very active organizers. Although they were arrested the unrest continued and reached a climax with a general strike on 10 March. The Tsar telegraphed orders from the front that the city authorities should immediately bring these disorders to an end. He added that the Duma should be dismissed. Clearly as far out of touch with the true situation as ever, Nicholas now had no Witte or Stolypin, or even a Rasputin, to rescue him. On 12 March the soldiers of the Petrograd garrison went over to the strikers. The police were overwhelmed and the Peter–Paul fortress was stormed. The workers' leaders were liberated and a new Soviet of Workers' and Soldiers' Deputies was set up. The Tsar's ministers begged to be dismissed from office and the Duma set up an emergency committee to carry on the government. Nicholas himself set out for his capital but his train was turned back on 13 March when it was learned that the line to Petrograd lay in revolutionary hands. In Petrograd, on 14 March, the Soviet agreed to support a Provisional Government formed from the Duma under the leadership of Prince Lvov, chairman of the National Union of Zemstvos.

This government now declared a total amnesty for political offenders and an unrestricted freedom of speech, association, and strike activity which would apply even to the armed forces. The police were to be replaced forthwith by a People's Militia and a Constituent Assembly was to be elected by universal suffrage to decide the political future of Russia. On 15 March representatives of the new government travelled to meet the Tsar and receive his abdication. He declined to hand on the crown to his ailing son but nominated his brother the Grand Duke Michael to take his place. Michael, after discussing the situation with the new government, declined to rule and Russia became a republic.

In this way the Romanov autocracy, which had ruled Russia for just over 300 years, collapsed in little more than three days. The speed and suddenness of the collapse is almost incredible and took all Russia by surprise. It is important to realize that the revolution had been confined almost entirely to the arena of Petrograd. The mood of the empire as a whole remained uncertain, although peasants were beginning to rise against their landlords. This land question was only one of the problems which now confronted the Provisional Government, thrust into the seat of power after ten years of inadequate inexperience. It had proved astonishingly easy to end the rule of tsardom but it was much more difficult to decide what should take its place. Prince Lvov and his advisers, understandably but perhaps unwisely, chose to defer their problems for as long as possible. They postponed the elections for the Constituent Assembly, put off a decision on the land question and announced their intention of continuing the war. At the same time however they abolished the death penalty for desertion, a step which proved fatal to military discipline. Once again their motive can be understood. They could not be sure of the attitude of the armed forces either at the front or in the capital. They were also bound to cast nervous glances over their shoulder at the Petrograd Soviet and the soviets which were springing up in other cities. The soviets' influence among the soldiers and the people was almost certainly greater than their own. The Petrograd Soviet was equally hesitant however. Alexander Kerensky, its Menshevik vice-president, was also a member of the Provincial

62 [opposite] A demonstration of workers in Petrograd in 1917, carrying slogans of the Bolshevik party: 'Down with War!', 'Down with the capitalist ministers!', and 'All Power to the Soviets!'

Government and used his influence to continue the uneasy alliance between the two bodies. Other members of the soviet were less willing to co-operate with the aristocratic government. A third element in this confused situation was Lenin, who now returned from exile in Switzerland in a sealed train provided by the German High Command. The Germans astutely realized that Lenin's arrival upon the revolutionary scene was certain to increase the confusion and weaken further the Russian war-effort.

And this it did. Arriving at the Finland Station in Petrograd in April, Lenin immediately demanded an end to the war, a redistribution of land to the poorer peasants, and a revolutionary dictatorship of the soviets in place of the Provisional Government.

> Having begun the revolution it is necessary to strengthen and continue it. All power in the state, from top to bottom, from the remotest village to the last street in the city of Petrograd, must belong to the Soviets of Workers', Soldiers' and Peasants' Deputies.

The Bolsheviks took up the slogans of 'Peace', 'Land' and 'All power to the Soviets' and began to agitate for them at every opportunity. This agitation increased the tension between the Petrograd Soviet and its supporters and put pressure on its leaders to lessen their support for the Provincial Government and the war. In July the tension flared up into a new revolutionary outbreak which went beyond the control of Lenin himself. Against his advice, because he did not think that the time was yet ripe for independent action, soldiers, sailors of the Baltic fleet, and workers besieged the Soviet and demanded that the moderates within it should break their ties with the government and hand over power to the extremists. The government however was still able to command sufficient support among officers and soldiers at the front to bring them back to suppress the rising. Bands of officers attacked the Bolshevik headquarters and the offices of the Bolshevik newspaper *Pravda* and arrested Trotsky and other party-leaders. Lenin fled once again to Finland.

Nevertheless the Petrograd Soviet now split from Prince Lvov and chaos was averted only by the appointment of Kerensky as head of government and minister for war. At the same time the Russian offensive at the front turned into defeat. Brusilov was replaced as commander-in-chief by General Kornilov, a man with sympathies neither for Kerensky nor the revolutionaries. Kornilov decided to use his new position not only to restore capital punishment within the army but also to crush the soviets. When Kerensky hesitated to go so far Kornilov ordered his Cossacks to

63　The battleship *Aurora*, moored in the Neva, bombarded the Winter Palace until the Provisional Government dissolved itself

march on Petrograd. In a desperate attempt to stop them the hapless Kerensky swung back to the Bolsheviks. Trotsky was released from prison and the 'Red Guards' of rebel soldiers and sailors were re-armed. Bolshevik agitators were sent out to meet the advancing counter-revolutionaries and spread anti-war propaganda among them. They did so successfully and Kornilov's threat to the capital melted away.

Although Kerensky now appointed himself commander-in-chief, he barely possessed an army to command. At the front the army was disintegrating in headlong retreat from the Germans. In Petrograd, Moscow, and the provincial cities the Bolsheviks used their second chance to increase their influence, persistently demanding an end to the war and the overthrow of the Provisional Government. They obtained a majority within the Petrograd Soviet and Trotsky became its president. An All-Russian Congress of Soviets was due to meet in the city in the first week of November and they were certain to enjoy a majority in that body also. Kerensky's only

hope lay in the Constituent Assembly, for which he ordered elections to be held at the end of the month.

Viewing these events from his hiding-place in Finland, Lenin concluded that the critical moment had arrived. To strike now would maximize Bolshevik power. To wait longer might be fatal. The Constituent Assembly was almost certain to be dominated by Social Revolutionaries who would never consent to a Bolshevik monopoly of power. Elsewhere in the provinces pro-Tsarist forces were already emerging after the first shock of the revolution. On the night of 6–7 November therefore Trotsky, from his headquarters in the Smolny Institute, a former girls' school, directed a well-planned and almost bloodless seizure of power by the Red Guards. The Tauride Palace, seat of the Duma, the National Bank, the railway stations, post offices, telephone exchanges, and power stations were occupied before dawn. Only the Winter Palace from which Kerensky ruled held out, defended by a handful of officer cadets and a women's regiment. The guns of the fortress of Saints Peter and Paul and the battleship *Aurora*, moored in the Neva, bombarded it with blank ammunition throughout the day and on 8 November the defenders capitulated. Kerensky disappeared in a motor-car loaned by the United States embassy. On the evening of 7 November Lenin emerged to address the Congress of Soviets for its opening session and announced that all power had passed to them. It would be administered by a Council of People's Commissars with himself at his head, Trotsky in charge of foreign affairs, and the Georgian Stalin as commissar for nationalities. The congress approved and Lenin announced his first decrees. Landlord property was abolished forthwith and negotiations would begin immediately for peace with the Germans.

Lenin's seizure of power in Petrograd, soon followed by a similar coup in Moscow, was far from being the end of the Russian revolution. There remained still the Constituent Assembly to be dealt with which, when it finally assembled in January 1918, refused, as predicted, to sign away its powers to the Bolshevik dictatorship. The assembly was dismissed at gun-point, exactly as the first Duma had been except that the agents on this occasion were Red Guards. Parliamentary democracy in Russia went with it. There remained also the Germans, with whom Trotsky concluded peace

64 [*opposite*] In a Bolshevik painting, Red Guards pause to light a cigarette among the tattered relics of tsardom in the Winter Palace

only at the expense of signing away almost the whole of the historic western lands which the Tsars had coveted and fought over for so long. Finally there remained the last Tsar himself, a prisoner with his family but a rallying-point, so long as he lived, for millions of Russians outside Petrograd whose loyalty he still commanded. Tsarist generals such as Kornilov rallied the remnants of their forces in distant bases in the provinces and mounted a counter-revolution. Social Revolutionaries also rose in revolt and Russia's Western allies began to intervene in the hope of defeating the Bolsheviks and keeping Russia in the First World War. In prisoner-of-war camps beyond the Urals a Czech Legion had been recruited to fight against the central powers on the eastern front. Its journey west had already begun when the Bolsheviks ended Russia's participation in the war and the Legion began to fight the Bolsheviks for control of the Trans-Siberian Railway. In July 1918 it drew near to Ekaterinburg, where the royal family was held by the Bolsheviks. The Ekaterinburg Soviet passed sentence of death and Nicholas and probably all his family were butchered in a cellar. Tragic though their fate was, the last Romanovs were only a handful among the millions of victims of civil war and famine which swept over Russia in the next three years. The Bolsheviks, now calling themselves Communists, eventually became masters of a ruined land.

Nevertheless, and although he himself did not survive for more than a few years longer, Lenin had won his long contest with Nicholas II. Communists tend to claim that his victory was the inevitable consequence of the logic of history which Marx had been the first to discover. The story of the confused events of 1917 suggests a more complex explanation however, in which both luck and judgment played essential parts. Lenin himself probably came nearer to the truth when he wrote, after the revolution, that

> The art of politics (and the Communist's correct understanding of his tasks) lies in correctly gauging the conditions and the moment when the vanguard of the proletariat can successfully seize power. . . .

Prompted, it is true, by his own unshakable faith in the logic of Marxism, this is what he had triumphantly achieved while the Provisional Government and the non-Bolshevik Socialists had fumbled for principles and policies on which to act.

The contrast with Nicholas's actions is even more striking. 'Is it possible', the Tsar had asked, shortly before his abdication, 'that for twenty-two years I tried to act for the best, and that for twenty-two years it was all a mistake?'

65 Still happiest on the land, but now in captivity.
Nicholas and his daughters work in the grounds
of their country residence in the first months after
the Tsar's deposition

His companion, the speaker of the Duma, had agreed that it was so. The Tsar's refusal to trust either the Duma or Witte, his submission to the will of Alexandra and perhaps of Rasputin, his final reluctant decision to precipitate the war and then to leave the capital for the front, all seem in retrospect to have been fatal errors. In everything he did, however, Nicholas had been true to his upbringing and to tsarist tradition. He sought to rule as the benevolent and autocratic father of his people and, in a war fought for traditional tsarist objectives, he took his natural place at the head of his fighting forces. A suggestion of inevitability thus clings to his fate more closely than to the victory of Lenin. For a century the gap between the Tsar and the people had grown increasingly wider under the tensions of economic and social change until, in the end, authority had come to rest on little more than military force and sentimental loyalty, both of which dissolved under the stress of the First World War.

Not everything that was characteristically tsarist disappeared with the Tsars, however, perhaps because what remained was also characteristically Russian. The Communists won the Civil War by establishing a military and political dictatorship. After the war they maintained this dictatorial power and institutionalized it in a party bureaucracy and a political police. When Stalin succeeded Lenin he restored collective farming, state control of industry and even military colonies. He repressed non-Russian nationalities and ruled through censorship, arrest, deportation, and execution. Almost immediately Russia set out to regain the western lands and, although she was baulked at first by military weakness, in 1939 Stalin concluded with Hitler a new partition of Poland. After the Second World War he extended Russian frontiers even further into eastern and central Europe. His successors put a Russian fleet on the Mediterranean. Communist Russia became the object of fear and suspicion in the West.

To a very great extent, of course, this fear sprang from new reasons. The new Russia, the Soviet Union, was dedicated to the destruction of capitalism, parliamentary democracy, and religion. To a very great extent, also, it was regarded differently by the Russian people themselves. In terms of health, education, social justice, and, eventually, of living standards Communist Russia was a new society. When Hitler's armies invaded Russia in 1941 however it was the old Russian patriotism, fierce and sacrificial, which they encountered and the Russian winter which again destroyed the invaders while Stalin, like Alexander I, fled from his capital. Many things changed in Russia under Communism but many remained unchanging.

66   The end of the empire of the Tsars: the
Bolshevik Trotsky arrives at Brest-Litovsk in 1918
to surrender all Russia's historic European conquests
to the Germans

The history of Communist Russia belongs to the twentieth century and,
viewed in that context, it represents a unique historical development in
the history of the world. Seen through the perspective of the nineteenth
century however it appears rather as one phase in the pattern of centuries
for a noble and tragic country.

Acknowledgements

The AUTHOR and PUBLISHERS wish to record their grateful thanks to copyright owners for the use of the illustrations listed below:

The Mansell Collection for: 1, 12, 22, 47, 48, 49, 52

Novosti Press Agency for: 10, 11, 16, 18, 28, 30, 33, 35, 36, 41, 43, 53, 54, 56, 61, 62, 63, 64, 66

Paul Popper Ltd for: 3, 5, 25, 60, 65

The Radio Times Hulton Picture Library for: 7, 9, 13, 14, 15, 17, 19, 21, 23, 27, 31, 32, 34, 38, 40, 44, 45, 46, 50, 55, 57, 58, 59

To S. C. R. Photo Library for: 2, 4, 6, 8, 20, 24, 26, 29, 37, 39, 42, 51

Index

Printed in Great Britain
by Jarrold & Sons Limited
Norwich